## MathFlare

**Name:** _______________________

**Class:** __________

**Teacher:** _______________________

# Introduction

As parents and educators, we recognize the pivotal role mathematics plays in shaping a child's academic journey and future success. Yet, the path to mathematical proficiency can often seem daunting, fraught with challenges and complexities. That's where the transformative power of MathFlare Workbooks shine through, illuminating the way forward with clarity, precision, and purpose.

Introducing MathFlare Workbooks – a beacon of guidance, a testament to excellence, and a catalyst for achievement. Crafted with meticulous care and expertise, MathFlare Workbooks stand as paragons of educational excellence, designed to nurture young minds, ignite a passion for learning, and develop a deep-rooted understanding of mathematical concepts.

Picture this: your child eagerly delves into the pages of Mathflare Workbook, greeted by a step-by-step guide illuminated with vivid examples that demystify complex mathematical concepts. With each turn of the page, they embark on a journey of discovery, encountering thoughtfully curated practice questions that reinforce learning and hone problem-solving skills. And when they unveil the answers to those very questions, a sense of accomplishment blossoms within them – a tangible reward for their hard work and dedication.

But MathFlare Workbooks are more than just tools for learning; they are pathways to comprehension, fostering a deep-seated understanding of mathematical concepts through a sequential, logical flow. From fundamental principles to advanced problem-solving strategies, every chapter builds upon the last, ensuring a robust foundation upon which future knowledge can be constructed.

As parents, we yearn for nothing more than to see our children thrive, to witness the spark of inspiration ignited within them as they conquer academic challenges with confidence and poise. MathFlare Workbooks serve as partners in this noble endeavor, offering not just practice questions, but the keys to unlocking a world of opportunity.

And for teachers, MathFlare Workbooks stand as invaluable allies in the quest to cultivate mathematical proficiency in the classroom. With answers readily available, instructors can focus on guiding and nurturing their students, confident in the knowledge that MathFlare Workbooks provide a solid framework upon which to build.

In the pages of MathFlare Workbooks, we find not just the promise of academic excellence, but the seeds of a brighter tomorrow. So let us embrace the power of mathematics, let us champion the journey of learning, and let us pave the way for a generation of young minds poised to shape the world. With MathFlare Workbooks as our guide, the possibilities are infinite, and the future, bright.

# Table of Contents

MathFlare
Grade 2
MATH WORKBOOK
Step by Step Guide and Essential Practice with Answers
Addition Subtraction
Multiplication
Place Value and Expanded Notations
Geometry
MathFlare Publishing

MathFlare
Grade 2-3
MATH WORKBOOK
Step by Step Guide and Essential Practice with Answers
Addition Subtraction
Multiplication and Division
Place Value and Expanded Notations
Geometry
MathFlare Publishing

MathFlare
Grade 3
MATH WORKBOOK
Step by Step Guide and Essential Practice with Answers
Multiplication and Division
Decimals
Place Value and Expanded Notations
Fractions and Geometry
MathFlare Publishing

MathFlare
Grade 1
MATH WORKBOOK
Step by Step Guide and Essential Practice with Answers
Counting and Numbers
Addition and Subtraction
Place Value and Expanded Notations
Understanding Time
MathFlare Publishing

MathFlare
Grade 1-2
MATH WORKBOOK
Step by Step Guide and Essential Practice with Answers
Counting and Numbers
Addition and Subtraction
Place Value and Expanded Notations
Understanding Time
MathFlare Publishing

MathFlare
Grade 3-4
MATH WORKBOOK
Step by Step Guide and Essential Practice with Answers
Addition Subtraction
Multiplication Division
Place Value and Expanded Notations
Fractions and Geometry
MathFlare Publishing

MathFlare
Grade 4
MATH WORKBOOK
Step by Step Guide and Essential Practice with Answers
Addition Subtraction
Multiplication Division
Place Value and Expanded Notations
Fractions and Geometry
MathFlare Publishing

MathFlare
Grade 4-5
MATH WORKBOOK
Step by Step Guide and Essential Practice with Answers
Multiplication Division
Place Value and Expanded Notations
Fractions and Geometry
Unit Conversion
MathFlare Publishing

MathFlare
MATH WORKBOOK
5
Step by Step Guide and Essential Practice with Answers
Multiplication Division
Place Value and Expanded Notations
Fractions and Geometry
Unit Conversion
MathFlare Publishing

MathFlare
MATH WORKBOOK
5-6
Step by Step Guide and Essential Practice with Answers
Multiplication Division
Place Value and Expanded Notations
Fractions and Geometry
Units and Statistics
MathFlare Publishing

MathFlare
MATH WORKBOOK
6
Step by Step Guide and Essential Practice with Answers
Integers and Statistics
Arithmetic and Pre-Algebra
Fractions and Geometry
Ratio and Percentage
MathFlare Publishing

MathFlare
MATH WORKBOOK
6-7
Step by Step Guide and Essential Practice with Answers
Arithmetic and Pre-Algebra
Ratio, Percent Proportion
Geometry
Statistics
MathFlare Publishing

MathFlare
MATH WORKBOOK
7
Step by Step Guide and Essential Practice with Answers
Pre-Algebra
Ratio, Percent Proportion
Geometry
Statistics
MathFlare Publishing

MathFlare
MATH WORKBOOK
7-8
Step by Step Guide and Essential Practice with Answers
Pre-Algebra
Ratio, Percent Proportion
Geometry and Cartesian Plane
Statistics
MathFlare Publishing

MathFlare
MATH WORKBOOK
8-9
Step by Step Guide and Essential Practice with Answers
Pre-Algebra
Ratio, Proportion and Percentage
Linear Equations
Geometry and Cartesian Plane
MathFlare Publishing

MathFlare
MATH WORKBOOK
8
Step by Step Guide and Essential Practice with Answers
Pre-Algebra
Percentage
Linear Equations
Geometry
MathFlare Publishing

# Place Value and Expanded Notations

Place value tells us the value of a digit in a number based on where it's placed.

Imagine we have the number 2,735,987,647.52843. It has 15 digits.

Now, each digit holds a special place. Let's break down the number 2,735,987,647.52843:

- The digit 2 is in billions place. Its value is 2 × 1,000,000,000=2,000,000,000

- The digit 7 is in hundred millions place. Its value is 7 × 100,000,000=700,000,000

- The digit 3 is in the ten millions place. Its value is 3 × 1,000,000=30,000,000.

- The digit 5 is in the millions place. Its value is 5 × 1,000,000=5,000,000.

- The digit 9 is in the hundred thousands place. Its value is 9×100,000=900,000.

- The digit 8 is in the ten thousands place. Its value is 8×10,000=80,000.

- The digit 7 is in the thousands place. Its value is 7×1,000=7,000.

- The digit 6 is in the hundreds place. Its value is 6×100=600.

- The digit 4 is in the tens place. Its value is 4×10=40.

- The digit 7 is in the ones place. Its value is 7×1=7.

- The digit 5 is in the tenths place. Its value is $5 \times \frac{1}{10} = 0.5$.

- The digit 2 is in the hundredths place. Its value is $2 \times \frac{1}{100} = 0.02$.

- The digit 8 is in the thousandths place. Its value is $8 \times \frac{1}{1000} = 0.008$.

- The digit 4 is in the ten thousandths place. Its value is $4 \times \frac{1}{10,000} = 0.0004$.

- The digit 3 is in the hundred thousandths place. Its value is $3 \times \frac{1}{100,000} = 0.00003$.

When we add these values together, we find the value of the entire number:

$$2,000,000,000 + 700,000,000 + 30,000,000 + 5,000,000 + 900,000 + 80,000 + 7,000 + 600 + 40 + 7 + 0.5 + 0.02 + 0.008 + 0.0004 + 0.00003 = 2,735,987,647.52843$$

**Let's solve some problems:**

Place value of the underlined digit:

36,837,434.19<u>9</u>  =  9 thousandths

Expanded notations:

802,278,509 — 8 hundred millions + 2 millions + 2 hundred thousands + 7 ten thousands + 8 thousands + 5 hundreds + 9 ones

# Rounding Numbers

Rounding numbers is the process of approximating a numerical value to a certain degree of accuracy by replacing it with a simpler or more convenient value. Rounding is commonly used to simplify calculations and express numbers in a more manageable form.

Steps to Rounding Numbers:

1.  **Identify the digit to be rounded:** Determine the digit to which the number will be rounded.

2.  **Look at the next digit:** Examine the digit immediately to the right of the one being rounded.

3.  **Decide whether to round up or down:** If the next digit is 5 or greater, round the digit up. If it is less than 5, round the digit down.

4.  **Adjust the number:** Change the digit being rounded and replace all digits to the right with zeros if necessary.

Properties of Rounding Numbers:
1.  **Accuracy:** Rounding reduces the precision of a number but maintains its approximate value.

2.  **Simplicity:** Rounding simplifies calculations by using fewer digits.

3.  **Ease of Use:** Rounding makes numbers easier to work with, especially in mental arithmetic and estimation.

Methods of Rounding Numbers:

1. **Round to Nearest Integer:** Round to the nearest whole number.

    I.    Round Up (Ceiling): Always round up to the nearest integer.

    II.   Round Down (Floor): Always round down to the nearest integer.

2. **Round to Nearest Tenth:** Round to the nearest tenth (one decimal place).

3. **Round to Nearest Hundredth:** Round to the nearest hundredth (two decimal places).

4. **Round to Nearest Thousandth:** Round to the nearest thousandth (three decimal places).

5. **Round to Specific Decimal Places:** Round to a specified number of decimal places as needed.

Let's round the number **438,576.214** to various degrees of accuracy:

| Rounding Level | Rounded Number | Difference from Original |
|---|---|---|
| Nearest Whole Number | 438,576 | 0 |
| Nearest Ten | 438,580 | +4 |
| Nearest Hundred | 438,600 | +24 |
| Nearest Thousand | 439,000 | +424 |
| Nearest Ten Thousand | 440,000 | +3,424 |
| Nearest Hundred Thousand | 400,000 | −38,576 |
| Nearest Million | $0.4386 \times 10^6$ | −438,576.214 |

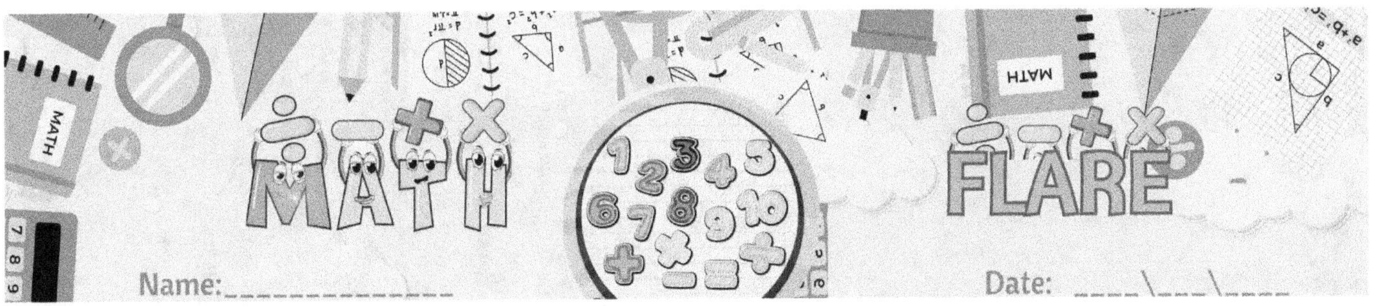


# Place Value

Determine the place value of the underlined digit.

1. 2,790,7<u>6</u>4,432.558 = _______________________________

2. 2,342,507,8<u>9</u>5.076 = _______________________________

3. 4,<u>0</u>18,353,467.017 = _______________________________

4. 7,153,386,956.43<u>6</u> = _______________________________

5. 2,55<u>1</u>,853,076.625 = _______________________________

6. 5,284,075,<u>6</u>47.265 = _______________________________

7. 3,0<u>8</u>9,506,802.416 = _______________________________

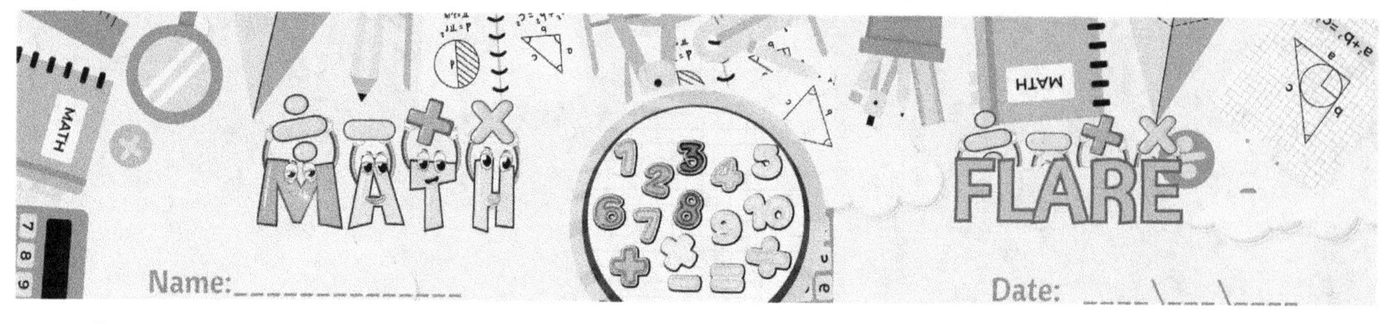


8. 4,350,63<u>9</u>,232.697 = _______________________________

9. 8,480,892,01<u>9</u>.256 = _______________________________

10. 9,924,870,185.<u>5</u>26 = _______________________________

11. 1,646,245,242.<u>7</u>67 = _______________________________

12. 2,063,866,5<u>3</u>1.834 = _______________________________

13. 9,910,4<u>0</u>7,073.296 = _______________________________

14. 3,85<u>7</u>,680,329.204 = _______________________________

15. 7,299,177,631.<u>2</u>13 = _______________________________

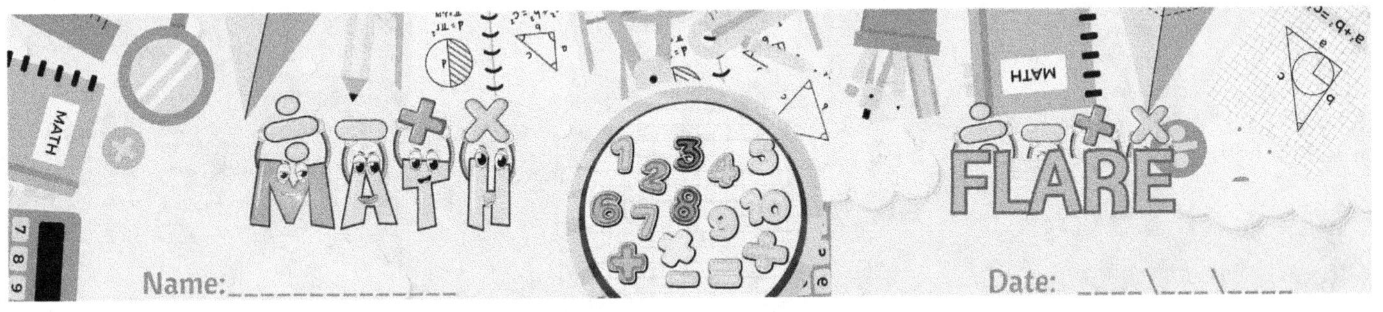


16. 6,2_73,053,842.165 = ________________________

17. 8,33_0,880,871.828 = ________________________

18. 1,532,552,90_2.75 = ________________________

19. 1,577,048,579._411 = ________________________

20. 7,996,3_76,319.986 = ________________________

21. 8,15_4,292,800.719 = ________________________

22. 9,9_62,688,196.901 = ________________________

23. 4,232,382,405._768 = ________________________

24. 5,295,734,287.847 = _______________________________

25. 8,944,280,125.745 = _______________________________

26. 4,036,946,615.352 = _______________________________

27. 1,460,285,026.251 = _______________________________

28. 4,487,651,992.902 = _______________________________

29. 5,078,025,090.105 = _______________________________

30. 9,899,607,732.854 = _______________________________

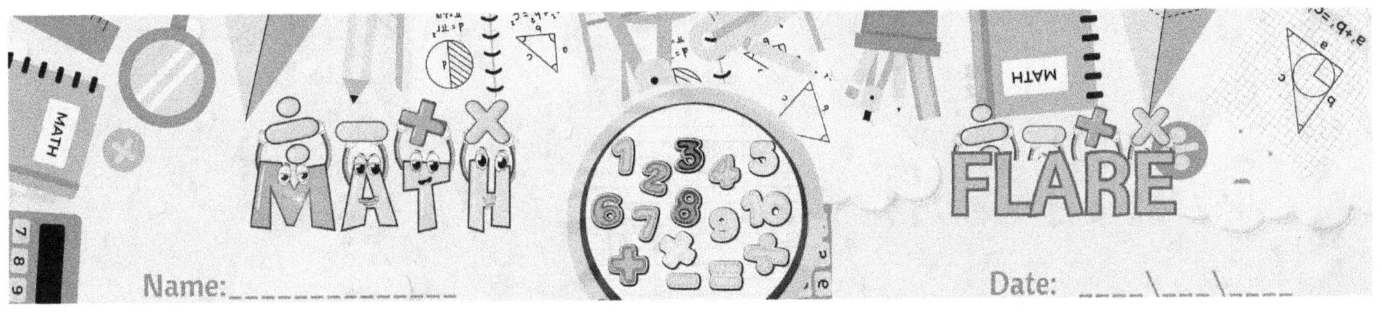


# Place Value: Expanded Notation

Provide the expanded notation for each value.

31. ___________________________

9 ten millions + 9 millions + 9 hundred thousands + 9 ten thousands + 7 thousands + 7 hundreds + 8 tens + 9 ones + 3 tenths + 1 hundredth + 4 thousandths

32. ___________________________

8 ten millions + 9 hundred thousands + 2 ten thousands + 1 thousand + 7 tens + 3 ones + 9 hundredths + 9 thousandths

33. ___________________________

4 ten millions + 8 millions + 8 hundred thousands + 7 ten thousands + 7 hundreds + 8 tens + 9 ones + 4 tenths + 8 hundredths + 2 thousandths

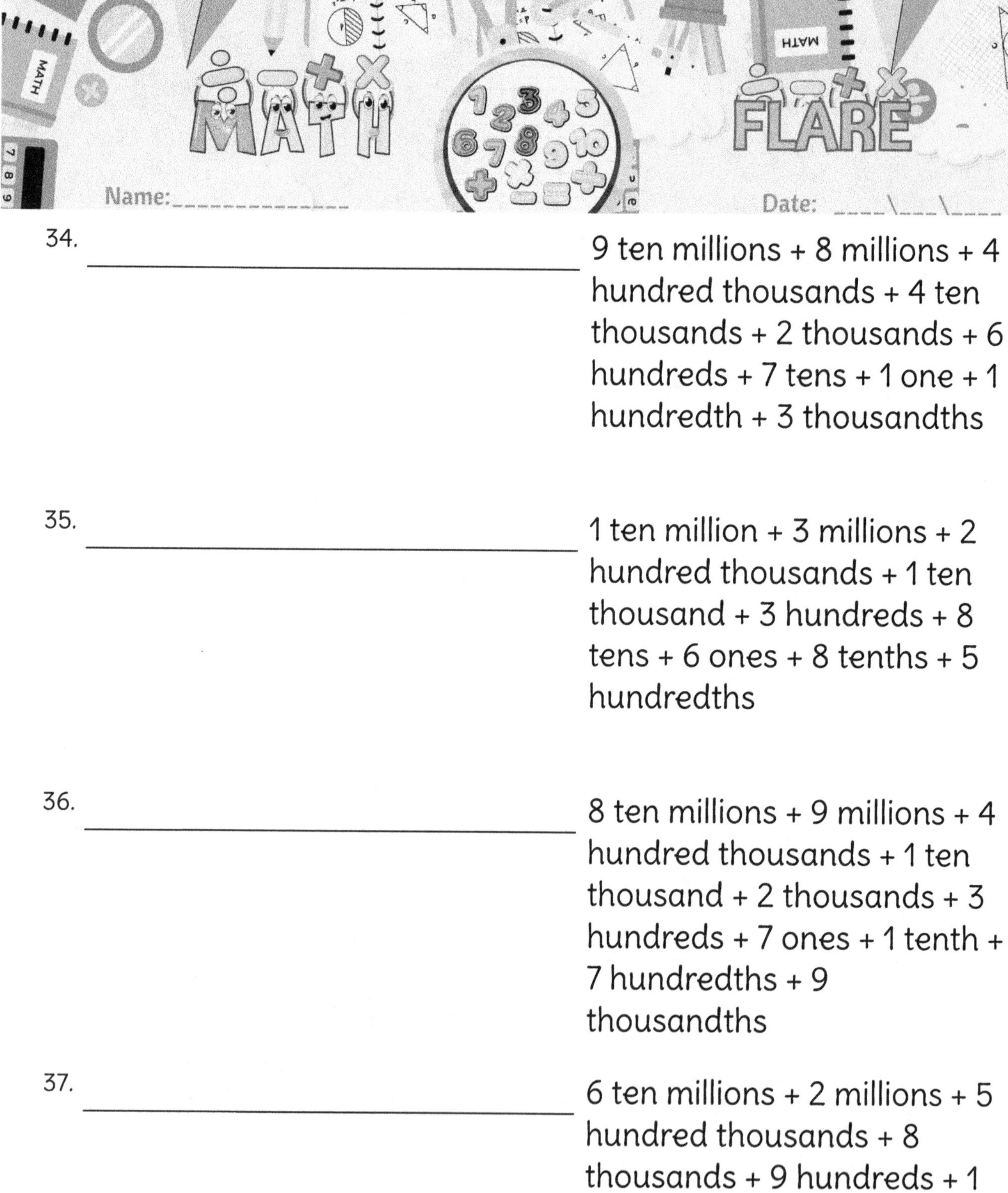

34. ____________________     9 ten millions + 8 millions + 4 hundred thousands + 4 ten thousands + 2 thousands + 6 hundreds + 7 tens + 1 one + 1 hundredth + 3 thousandths

35. ____________________     1 ten million + 3 millions + 2 hundred thousands + 1 ten thousand + 3 hundreds + 8 tens + 6 ones + 8 tenths + 5 hundredths

36. ____________________     8 ten millions + 9 millions + 4 hundred thousands + 1 ten thousand + 2 thousands + 3 hundreds + 7 ones + 1 tenth + 7 hundredths + 9 thousandths

37. ____________________     6 ten millions + 2 millions + 5 hundred thousands + 8 thousands + 9 hundreds + 1 one + 4 tenths + 9 hundredths + 3 thousandths

38. _______________________________  1 ten million + 1 million + 8 hundred thousands + 4 thousands + 6 hundreds + 2 tens + 2 ones + 2 tenths + 3 thousandths

39. _______________________________  9 ten millions + 3 millions + 4 hundred thousands + 4 ten thousands + 6 thousands + 7 hundreds + 1 ten + 9 ones + 8 tenths + 5 hundredths + 2 thousandths

40. _______________________________  2 ten millions + 7 hundred thousands + 3 ten thousands + 7 thousands + 2 hundreds + 8 tens + 2 ones + 8 hundredths + 9 thousandths

41. _______________________________  7 ten millions + 7 hundred thousands + 8 ten thousands + 8 thousands + 1 hundred + 8 tens + 3 ones + 2 tenths + 2 hundredths + 6 thousandths

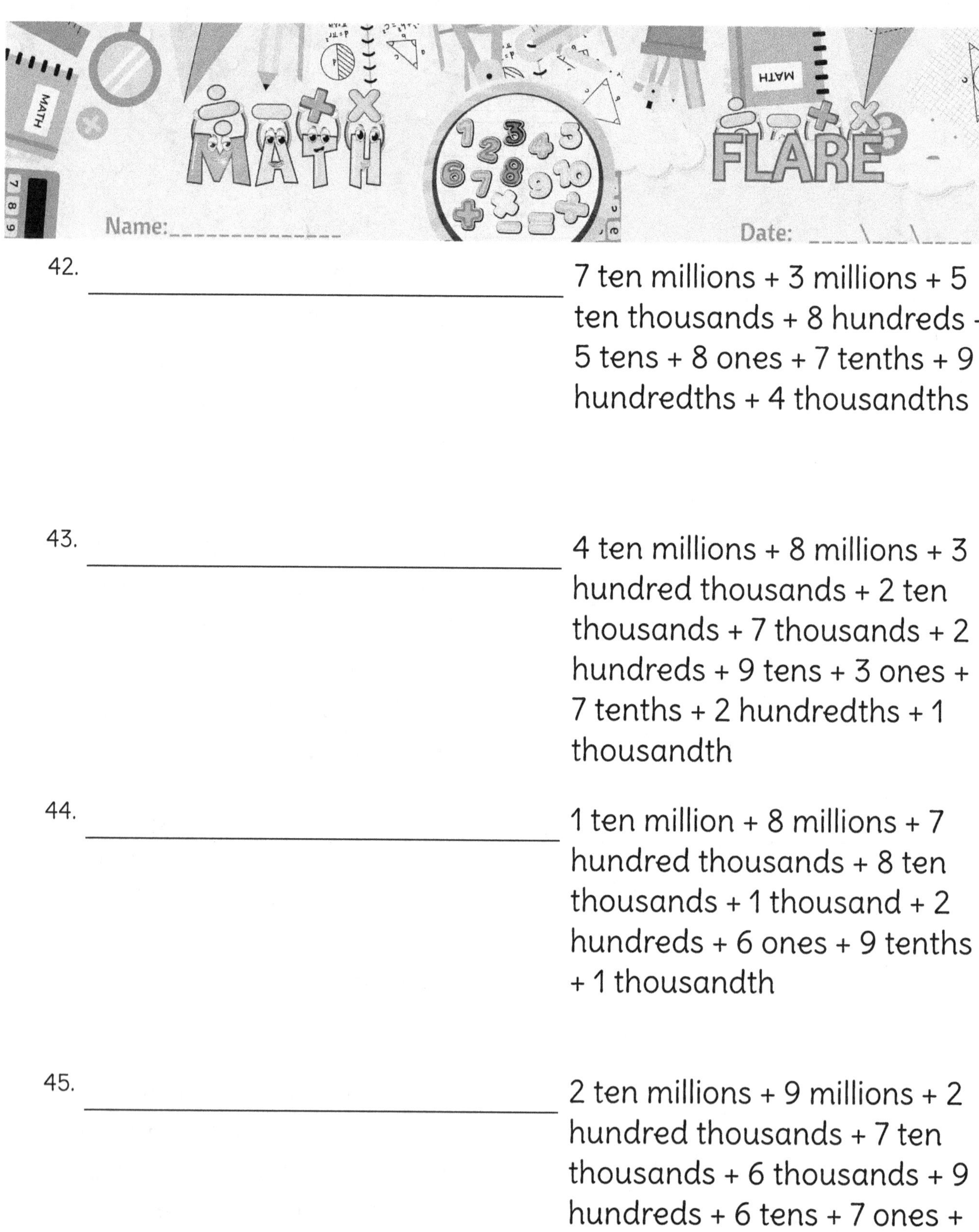



42. _______________________________

7 ten millions + 3 millions + 5 ten thousands + 8 hundreds + 5 tens + 8 ones + 7 tenths + 9 hundredths + 4 thousandths

43. _______________________________

4 ten millions + 8 millions + 3 hundred thousands + 2 ten thousands + 7 thousands + 2 hundreds + 9 tens + 3 ones + 7 tenths + 2 hundredths + 1 thousandth

44. _______________________________

1 ten million + 8 millions + 7 hundred thousands + 8 ten thousands + 1 thousand + 2 hundreds + 6 ones + 9 tenths + 1 thousandth

45. _______________________________

2 ten millions + 9 millions + 2 hundred thousands + 7 ten thousands + 6 thousands + 9 hundreds + 6 tens + 7 ones + 4 hundredths + 8 thousandths

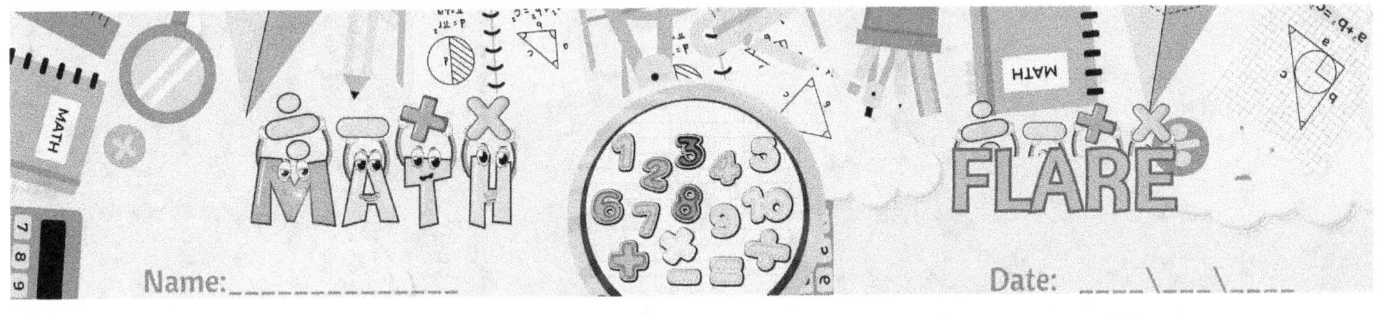


46. _________________________________  1 ten million + 6 millions + 1 hundred thousand + 6 ten thousands + 2 thousands + 9 hundreds + 6 tens + 4 ones + 5 tenths + 4 thousandths

47. _________________________________  3 ten millions + 6 millions + 5 ten thousands + 2 thousands + 5 hundreds + 7 tens + 2 ones + 4 tenths + 8 hundredths + 3 thousandths

48. _________________________________  7 ten millions + 3 millions + 3 ten thousands + 5 hundreds + 1 one + 6 tenths + 2 hundredths + 3 thousandths

49. _________________________________  6 ten millions + 8 millions + 1 hundred thousand + 7 ten thousands + 8 thousands + 3 hundreds + 1 ten + 7 ones + 8 tenths + 2 hundredths + 9 thousandths

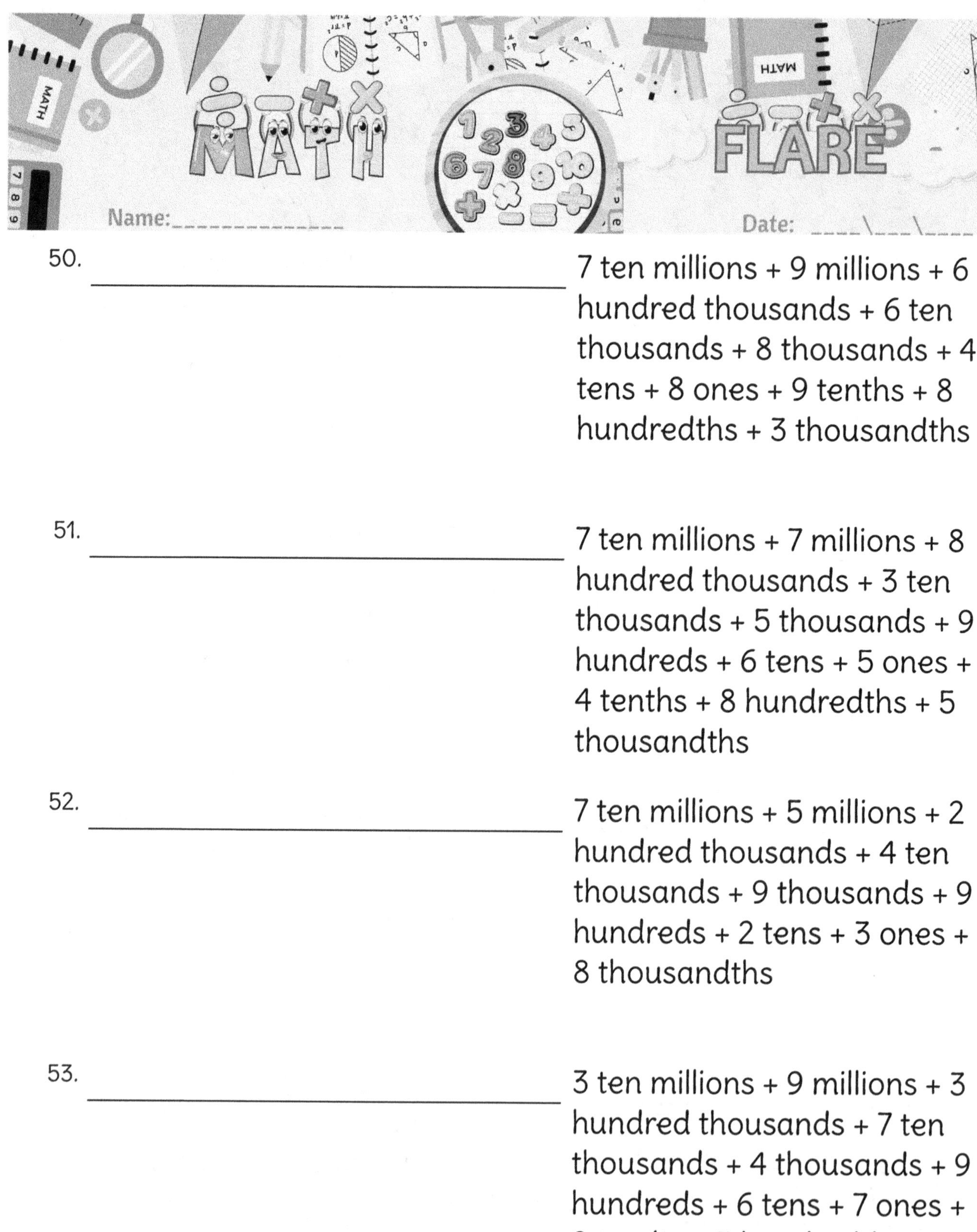



50. _______________________________

7 ten millions + 9 millions + 6 hundred thousands + 6 ten thousands + 8 thousands + 4 tens + 8 ones + 9 tenths + 8 hundredths + 3 thousandths

51. _______________________________

7 ten millions + 7 millions + 8 hundred thousands + 3 ten thousands + 5 thousands + 9 hundreds + 6 tens + 5 ones + 4 tenths + 8 hundredths + 5 thousandths

52. _______________________________

7 ten millions + 5 millions + 2 hundred thousands + 4 ten thousands + 9 thousands + 9 hundreds + 2 tens + 3 ones + 8 thousandths

53. _______________________________

3 ten millions + 9 millions + 3 hundred thousands + 7 ten thousands + 4 thousands + 9 hundreds + 6 tens + 7 ones + 8 tenths + 3 hundredths + 6 thousandths

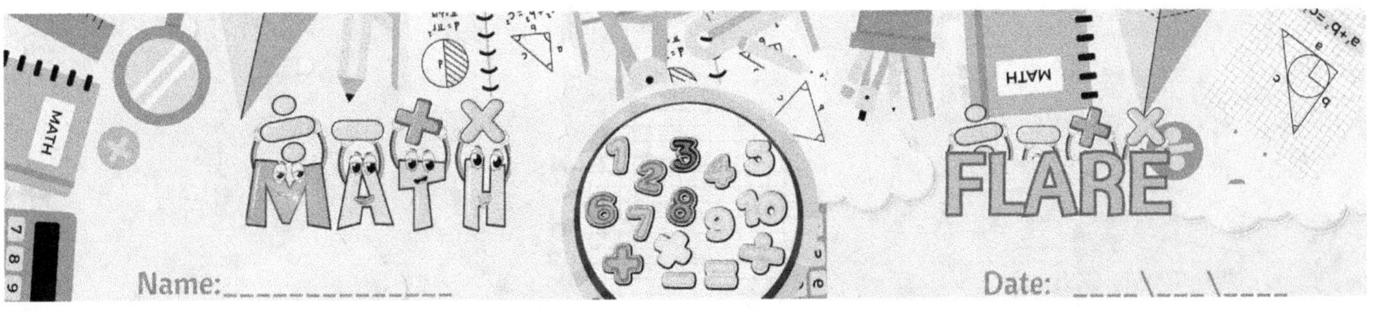


54. _______________________

5 ten millions + 3 millions + 1 ten thousand + 9 thousands + 7 hundreds + 3 tens + 1 one + 9 tenths + 3 hundredths + 5 thousandths

55. _______________________

7 ten millions + 7 millions + 6 ten thousands + 1 thousand + 6 hundreds + 7 tens + 5 ones + 6 tenths + 1 hundredth + 3 thousandths

56. _______________________

9 ten millions + 8 millions + 7 thousands + 3 hundreds + 5 tens + 3 ones + 5 tenths + 6 hundredths + 1 thousandth

57. _______________________

4 ten millions + 7 hundred thousands + 6 ten thousands + 4 thousands + 1 hundred + 5 tens + 7 ones + 2 tenths + 2 hundredths + 7 thousandths

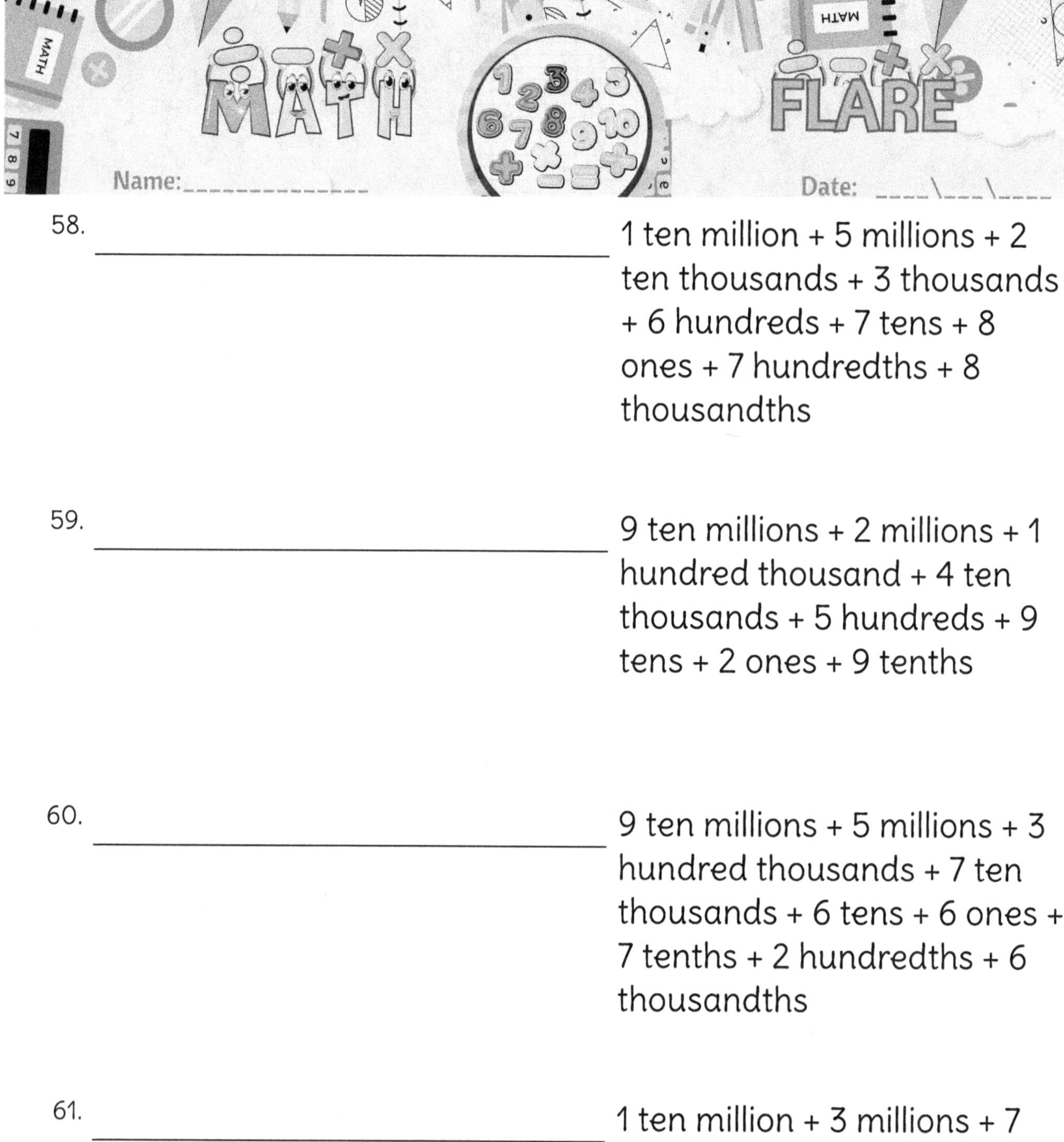



58. _______________________________

1 ten million + 5 millions + 2 ten thousands + 3 thousands + 6 hundreds + 7 tens + 8 ones + 7 hundredths + 8 thousandths

59. _______________________________

9 ten millions + 2 millions + 1 hundred thousand + 4 ten thousands + 5 hundreds + 9 tens + 2 ones + 9 tenths

60. _______________________________

9 ten millions + 5 millions + 3 hundred thousands + 7 ten thousands + 6 tens + 6 ones + 7 tenths + 2 hundredths + 6 thousandths

61. _______________________________

1 ten million + 3 millions + 7 ten thousands + 6 thousands + 7 hundreds + 5 tens + 7 ones + 1 hundredth + 7 thousandths

66. 14,404,810.106 _______________________________

67. 89,842,765.936 _______________________________

68. 26,285,007.399 _______________________________

69. 32,755,188.855 _______________________________

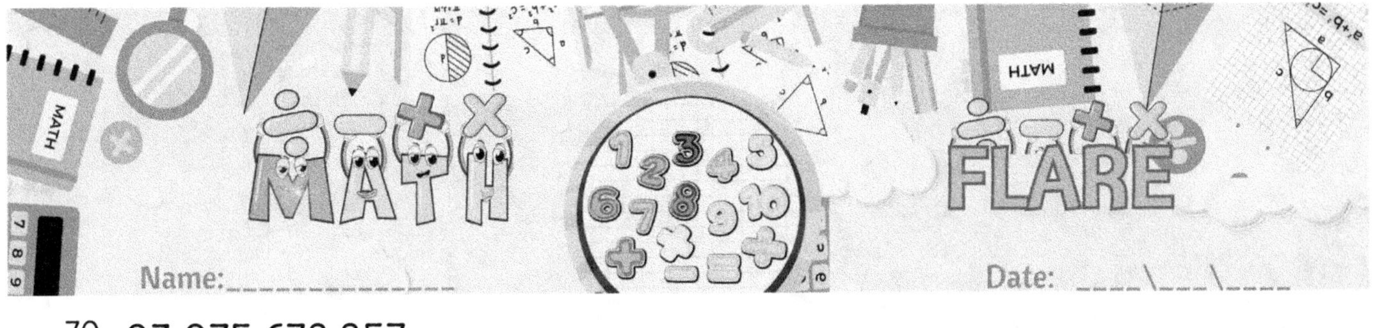


70. 93,075,678.857

71. 36,847,770.385

72. 41,876,914.260

73. 40,409,638.556

74. 17,543,480.260  _______________________

75. 20,313,071.664  _______________________

76. 24,175,332.996  _______________________

77. 43,763,774.584  _______________________

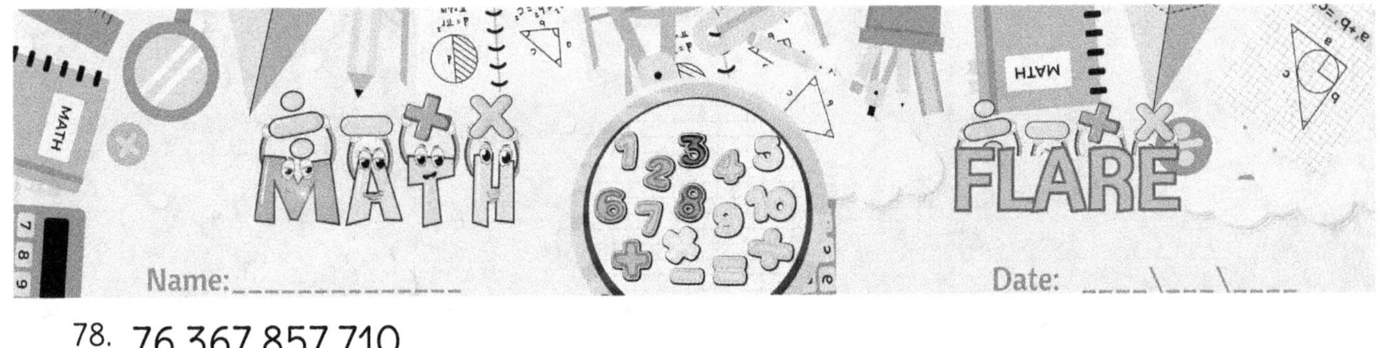


78. 76,367,857.710  ____________________________

79. 28,960,939.165  ____________________________

80. 79,855,583.589  ____________________________

81. 66,673,568.941  ____________________________

82. 22,782,341.238

83. 90,404,080.156

84. 67,769,682.573

85. 31,285,197.875

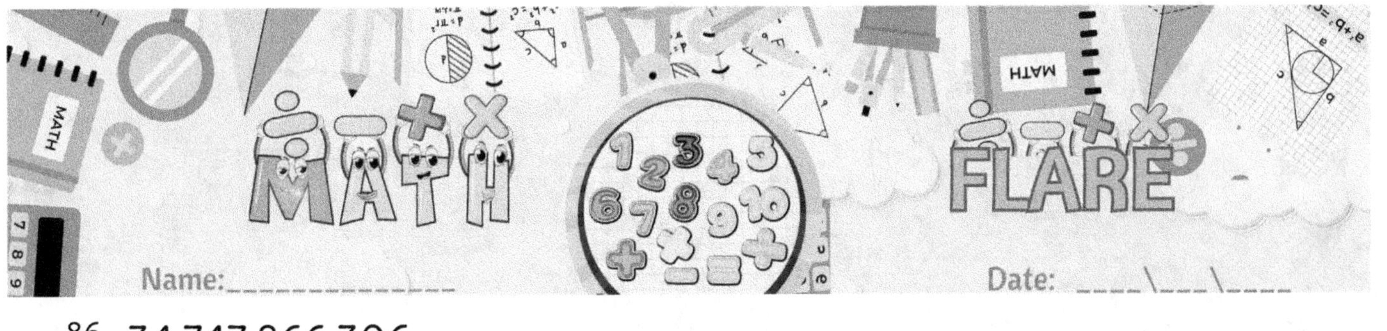


86. 34,747,866.306  _______________________

87. 51,546,105.263  _______________________

88. 95,851,057.546  _______________________

89. 31,380,995.401  _______________________

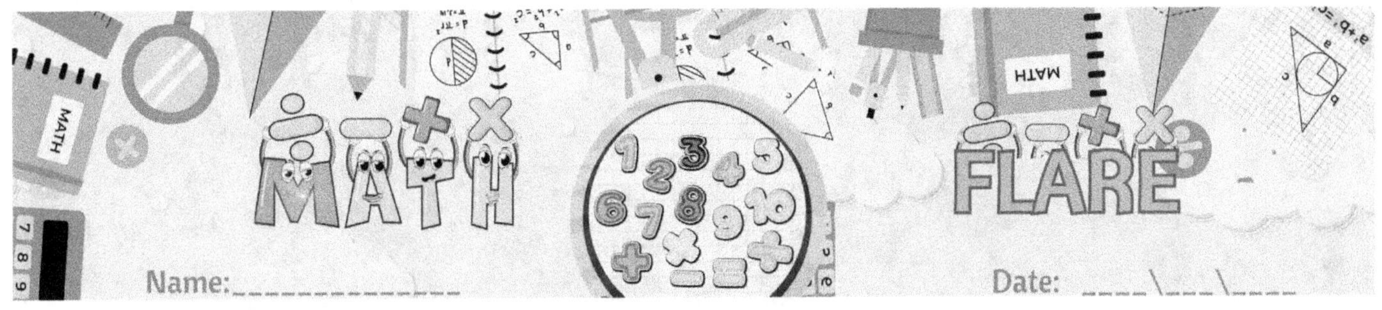


# Place Value: Expanded Notation

Provide the expanded notation for each value.

62. 22,953,242.838

63. 42,468,752.522

64. 51,994,344.173

65. 31,590,469.932

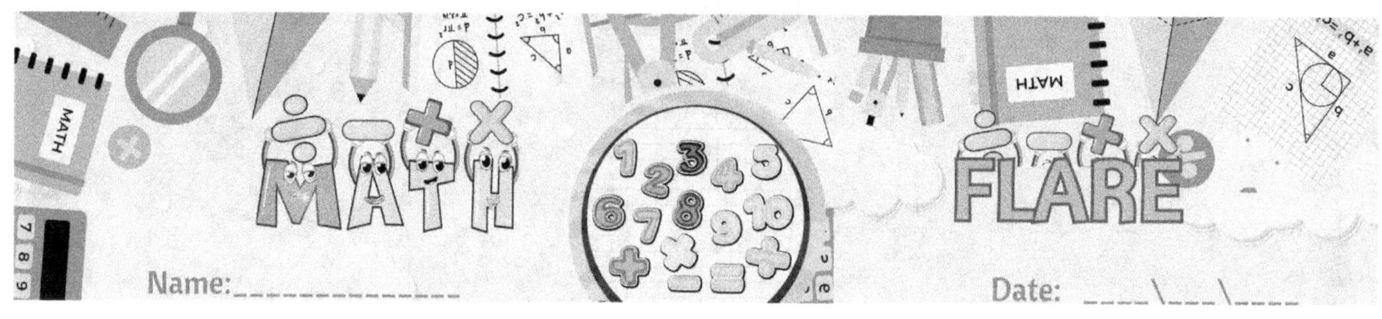


# Place Value: Expanded Notation

Provide the expanded notation for each value.

90. _________________________________

10,000,000 + 5,000,000 + 200,000 + 3,000 + 30 + 3 + 0.2 + 0.08 + 0.008

91. _________________________________

50,000,000 + 8,000,000 + 600,000 + 40,000 + 8,000 + 100 + 40 + 9 + 0.9 + 0.05 + 0.002

92. _________________________________

50,000,000 + 7,000,000 + 400,000 + 80,000 + 5,000 + 200 + 20 + 3 + 0.4 + 0.01 + 0.005

93. _________________________________

10,000,000 + 9,000,000 + 600,000 + 60,000 + 4,000 + 20 + 9 + 0.3 + 0.002

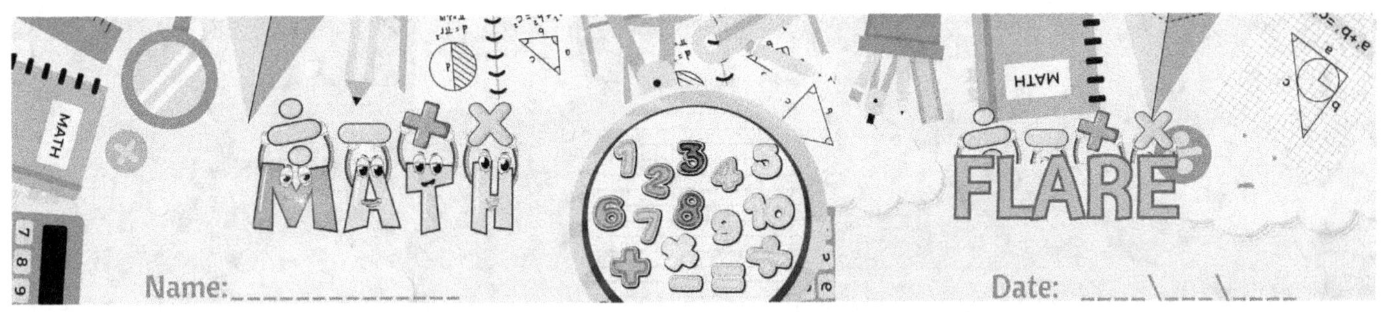


94. _______________________________
90,000,000 + 8,000,000 + 70,000 + 6,000 + 600 + 50 + 3 + 0.1 + 0.02 + 0.005

95. _______________________________
10,000,000 + 7,000,000 + 600,000 + 60,000 + 500 + 20 + 5 + 0.07 + 0.002

96. _______________________________
50,000,000 + 7,000,000 + 800,000 + 30,000 + 4,000 + 900 + 40 + 0.3 + 0.08 + 0.008

97. _______________________________
40,000,000 + 500,000 + 80,000 + 2,000 + 100 + 6 + 0.2 + 0.07 + 0.002

98. _________________________________   90,000,000 + 6,000,000 + 300,000 + 30,000 + 2,000 + 900 + 40 + 9 + 0.5 + 0.04 + 0.006

99. _________________________________   80,000,000 + 7,000,000 + 100,000 + 90,000 + 700 + 30 + 6 + 0.9 + 0.06 + 0.008

100. _________________________________   20,000,000 + 4,000,000 + 800,000 + 70,000 + 2,000 + 100 + 50 + 6 + 0.9 + 0.04 + 0.003

101. _________________________________   20,000,000 + 6,000,000 + 300,000 + 20,000 + 100 + 90 + 8 + 0.5 + 0.06 + 0.008

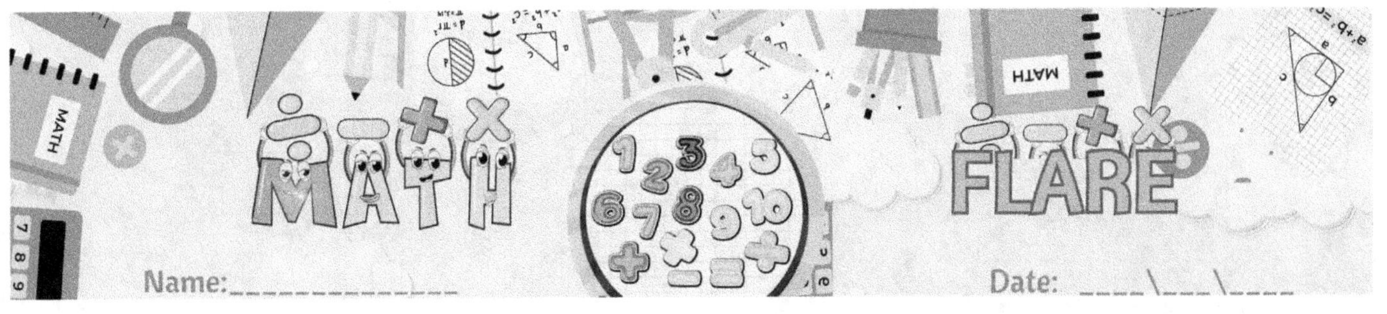


102. _______________________________  10,000,000 + 9,000,000 + 700,000 + 60,000 + 7,000 + 500 + 60 + 5 + 0.08 + 0.004

103. _______________________________  50,000,000 + 200,000 + 70,000 + 5,000 + 300 + 10 + 2 + 0.7 + 0.06 + 0.009

104. _______________________________  70,000,000 + 5,000,000 + 100,000 + 2,000 + 600 + 30 + 8 + 0.9 + 0.07 + 0.002

105. _______________________________  50,000,000 + 2,000,000 + 800,000 + 20,000 + 200 + 70 + 8 + 0.5 + 0.09 + 0.008

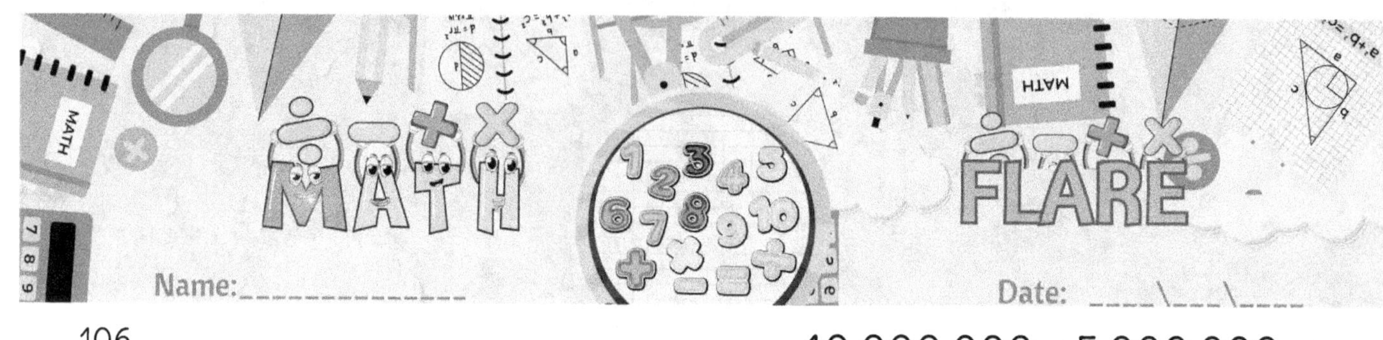


106. _______________________________

40,000,000 + 5,000,000 + 900,000 + 50,000 + 9,000 + 50 + 1 + 0.2 + 0.02 + 0.006

107. _______________________________

40,000,000 + 4,000,000 + 800,000 + 40,000 + 200 + 80 + 4 + 0.4 + 0.05 + 0.003

108. _______________________________

30,000,000 + 1,000,000 + 800,000 + 30,000 + 1,000 + 400 + 80 + 7 + 0.5 + 0.07 + 0.006

109. _______________________________

40,000,000 + 2,000,000 + 700,000 + 6,000 + 600 + 60 + 0.2 + 0.07 + 0.001

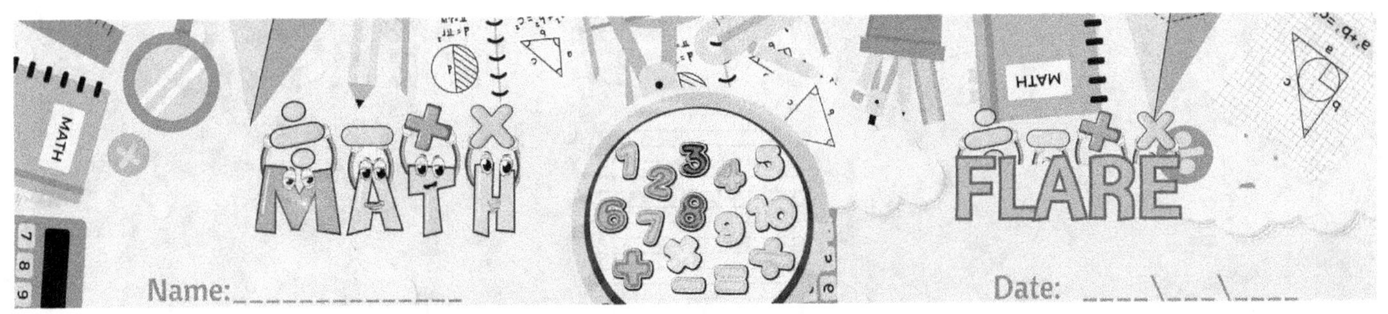


110. _______________________________

60,000,000 + 2,000,000 + 800,000 + 80,000 + 6,000 + 300 + 40 + 2 + 0.6 + 0.01 + 0.007

111. _______________________________

60,000,000 + 4,000,000 + 200,000 + 40,000 + 3,000 + 500 + 70 + 8 + 0.9 + 0.07 + 0.007

112. _______________________________

60,000,000 + 4,000,000 + 300,000 + 90,000 + 6,000 + 200 + 90 + 9 + 0.5 + 0.01 + 0.006

113. _______________________________

80,000,000 + 6,000,000 + 60,000 + 2,000 + 700 + 30 + 8 + 0.9 + 0.01 + 0.001

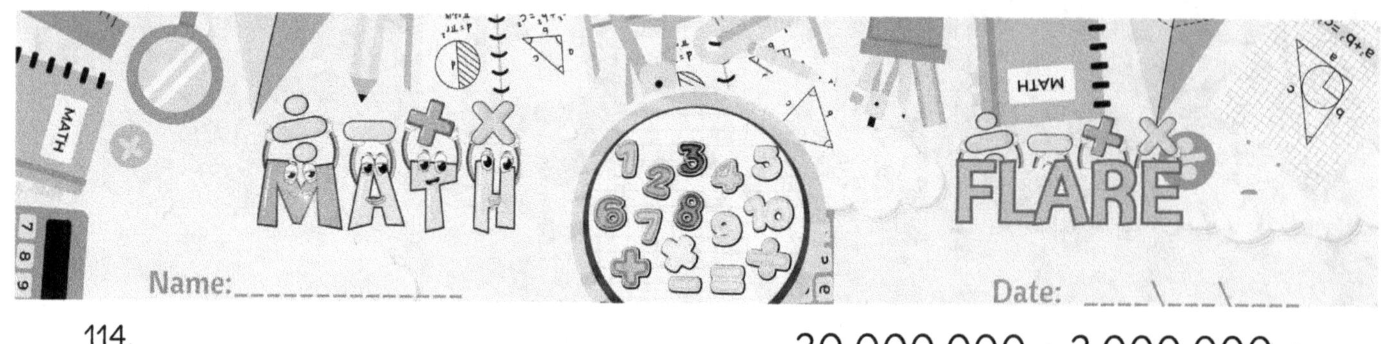


114. _______________________________

20,000,000 + 2,000,000 + 200,000 + 80,000 + 5,000 + 9 + 0.3 + 0.01 + 0.002

115. _______________________________

30,000,000 + 8,000,000 + 600,000 + 90,000 + 6,000 + 400 + 90 + 7 + 0.7 + 0.08 + 0.005

116. _______________________________

90,000,000 + 200,000 + 90,000 + 4,000 + 400 + 10 + 5 + 0.7 + 0.07 + 0.008

117. _______________________________

30,000,000 + 2,000,000 + 500,000 + 40,000 + 9,000 + 100 + 60 + 2 + 0.6 + 0.08

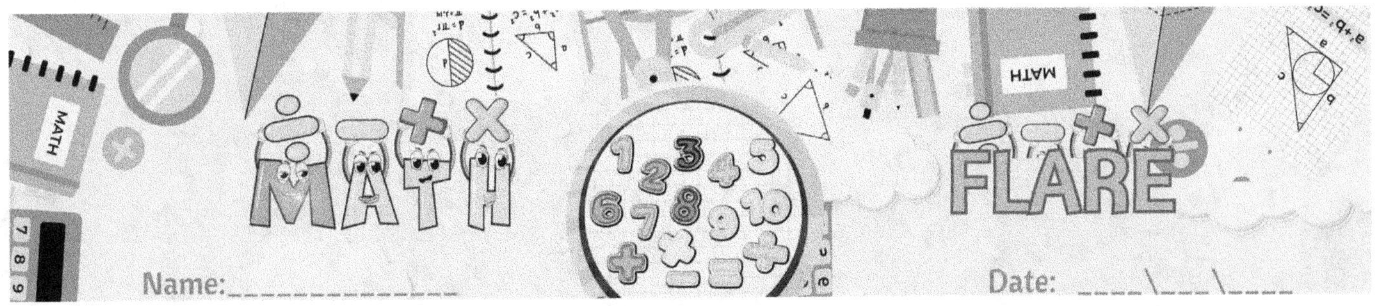


# Place Value: Expanded Notation

Provide the expanded notation for each value.

118. 7,469,906.994  ___________________________

119. 3,070,914.630  ___________________________

120. 9,684,260.362  ___________________________

121. 6,285,870.484  ___________________________

122. 9,399,170.838  ___________________________

123. 9,490,401.199 _______________

124. 2,755,215.557 _______________

125. 4,442,752.890 _______________

126. 7,936,254.696 _______________

127. 3,221,288.496 _______________

128. 4,233,298.543 _______________

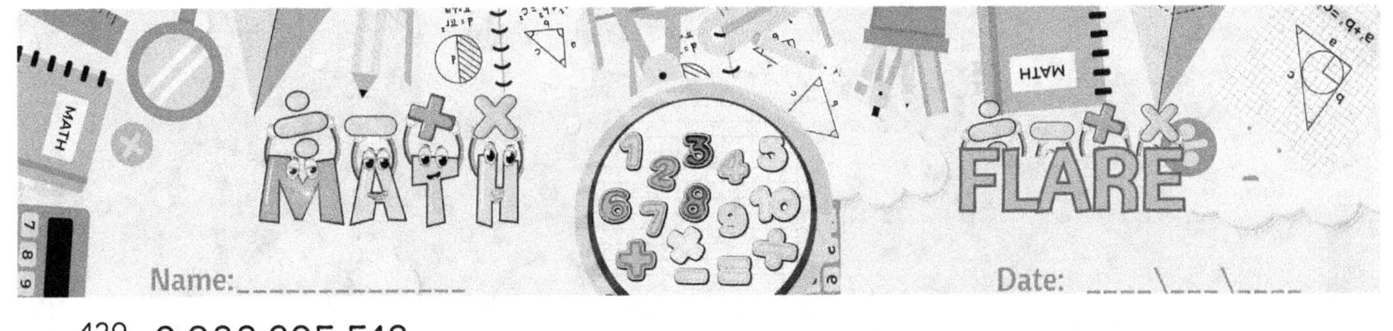


129. 9,988,295.518

130. 6,247,813.127

131. 8,359,322.672

132. 4,743,082.503

133. 8,917,712.073

134. 1,408,878.222

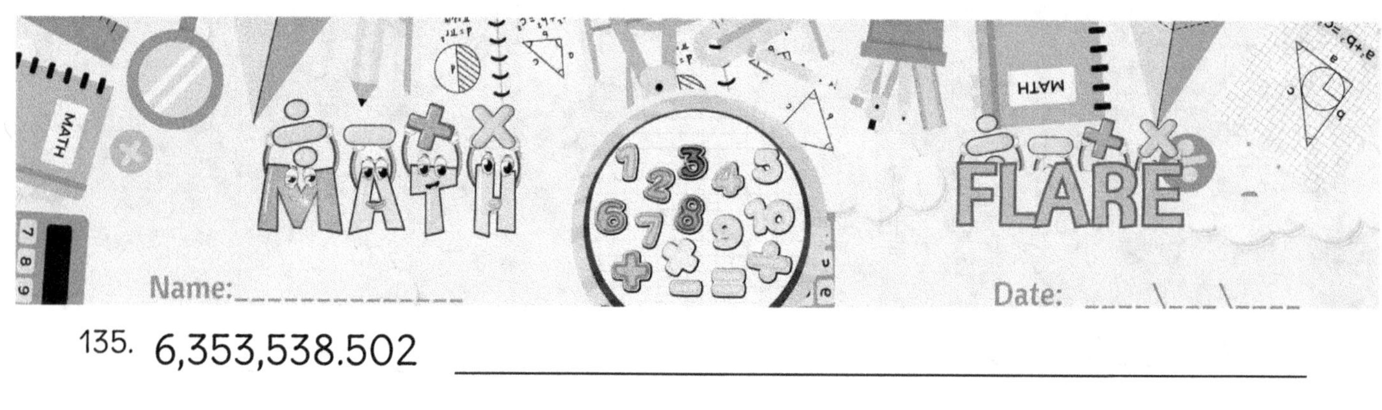


135. 6,353,538.502 ____________________

136. 5,690,600.385 ____________________

137. 7,250,702.846 ____________________

138. 2,530,144.118 ____________________

139. 2,494,940.397 ____________________

140. 8,532,614.664 ____________________

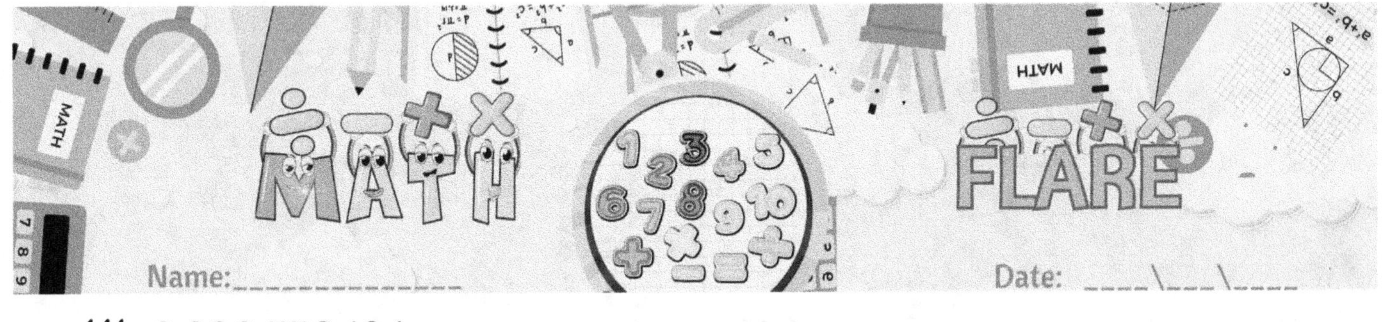


141. 8,990,758.184 _______________________

142. 2,971,461.768 _______________________

143. 6,314,439.727 _______________________

144. 6,849,465.278 _______________________

145. 5,095,945.431 _______________________

146. 9,425,185.043 _______________________

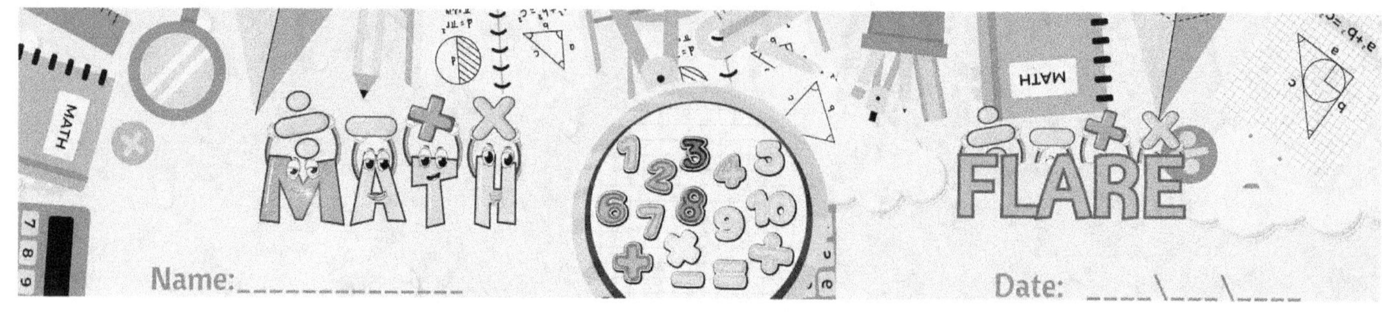


# Place Value: Expanded Notation

Provide the expanded notation for each value.

147. _________________________________ seventy-one million four hundred twenty-two thousand four hundred eighty-four and five hundred three thousandths

148. _________________________________ ninety-seven million three hundred seventy-nine thousand nineteen and nine hundred eighty-nine thousandths

149. _________________________________ sixty-nine million three hundred eighty thousand one hundred fifty-five and three hundred forty thousandths

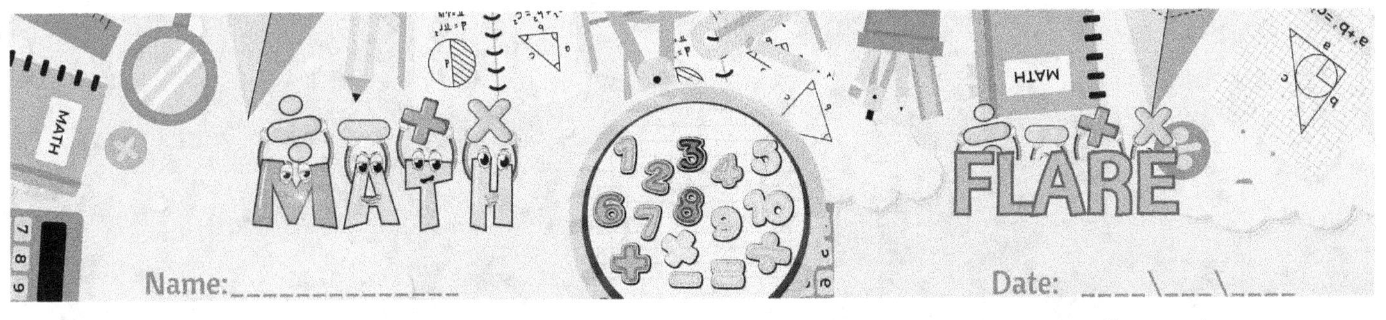


150. _______________________________  twenty-seven million three hundred sixty-six thousand one hundred nine and two hundred ninety-three thousandths

151. _______________________________  thirty-five million two hundred eighty-five thousand seven hundred seventy-seven and seven hundred eight thousandths

152. _______________________________  sixty-five million eight hundred eighty-three thousand thirty-six and three hundred twenty-three thousandths

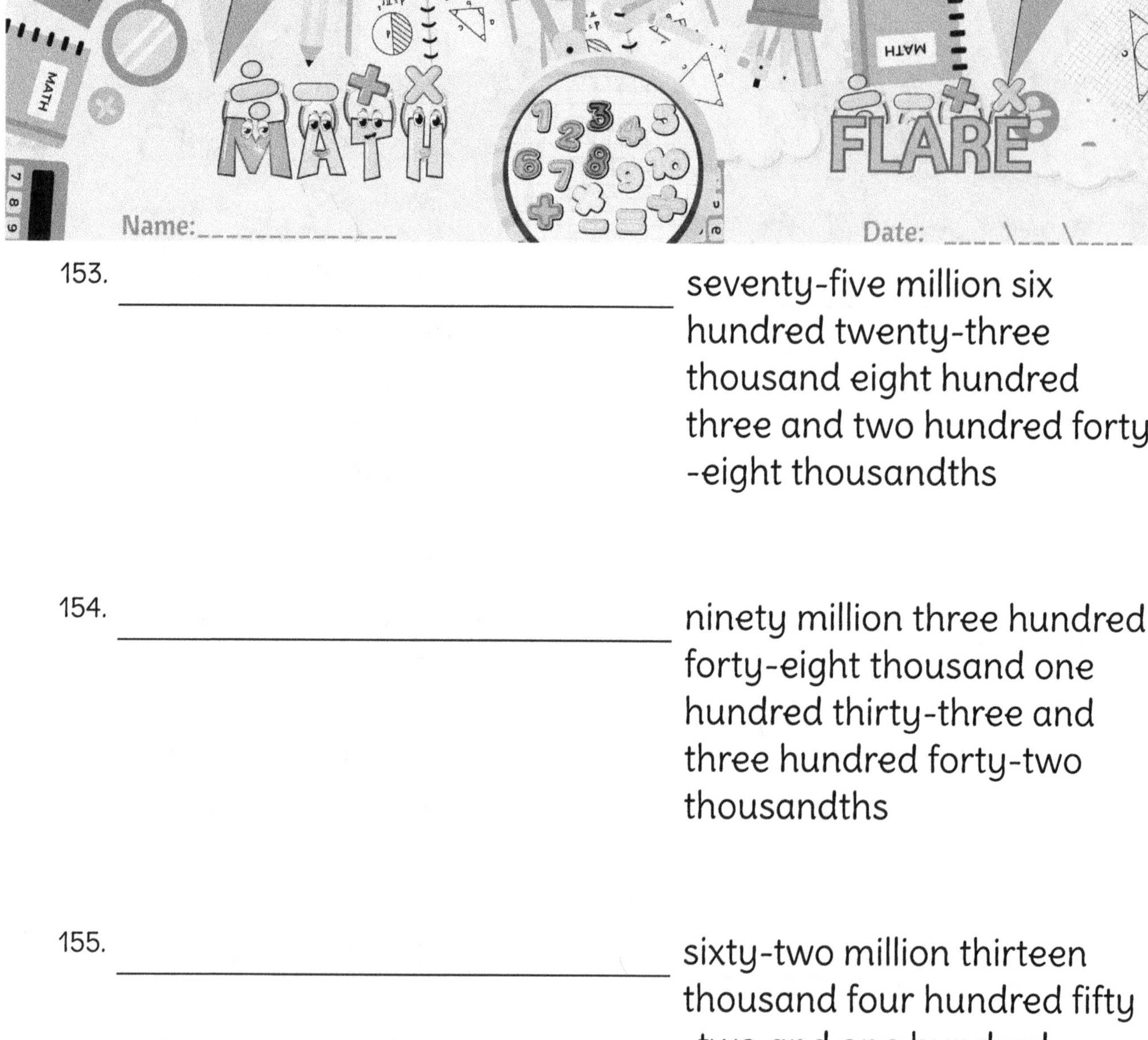


153. _______________________ seventy-five million six hundred twenty-three thousand eight hundred three and two hundred forty-eight thousandths

154. _______________________ ninety million three hundred forty-eight thousand one hundred thirty-three and three hundred forty-two thousandths

155. _______________________ sixty-two million thirteen thousand four hundred fifty-two and one hundred thousandth

156. _______________________  thirty-two million three hundred twenty-eight thousand four hundred ninety and one hundred seventy-eight thousandth

157. _______________________  twenty-four million eight hundred sixty-three thousand five hundred fifty-three and eighty-seven thousandths

158. _______________________  thirty-two million seven hundred twenty-three thousand one hundred fifty-seven and two hundred two thousandths

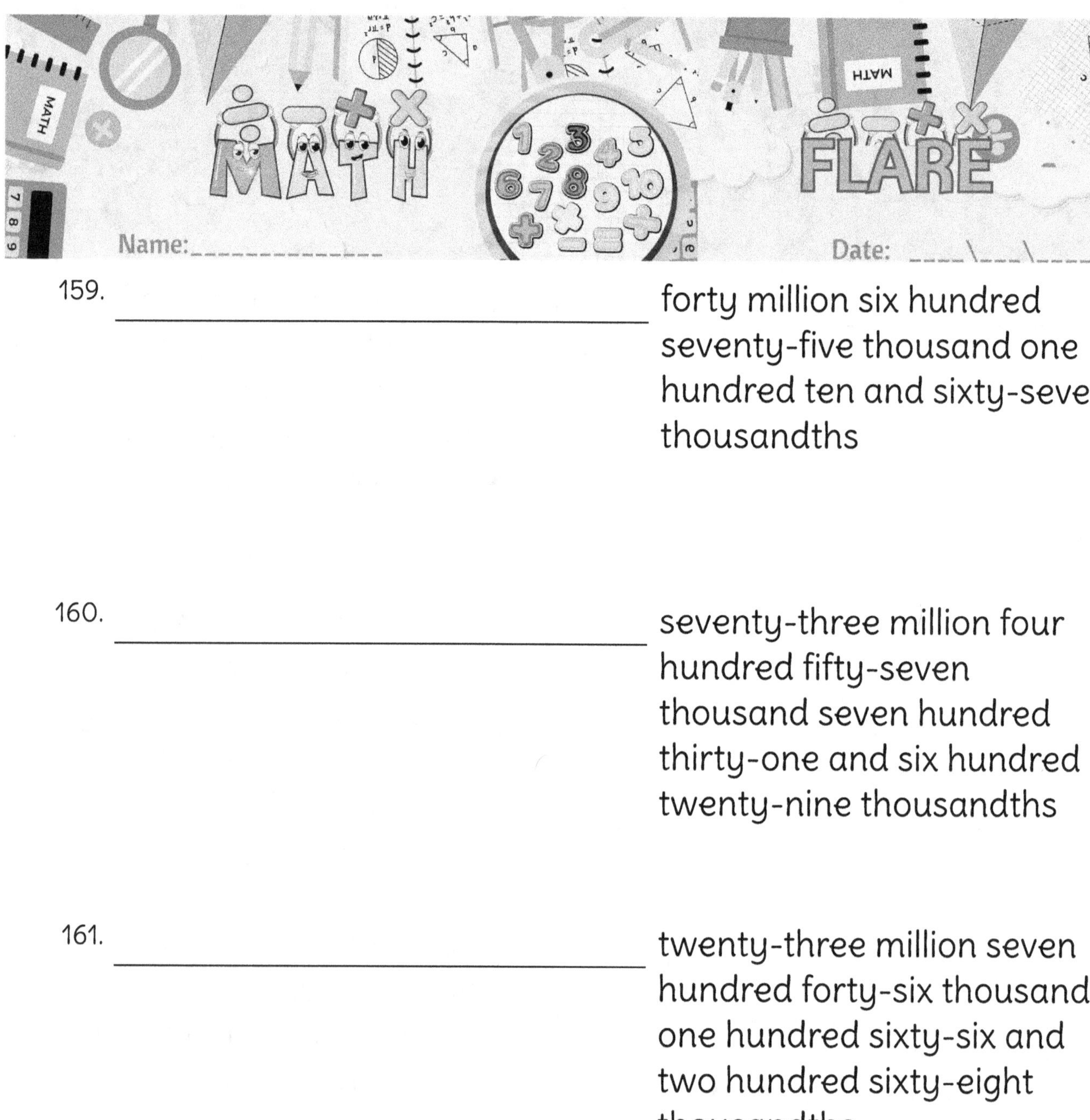

159. __________________________  forty million six hundred seventy-five thousand one hundred ten and sixty-seven thousandths

160. __________________________  seventy-three million four hundred fifty-seven thousand seven hundred thirty-one and six hundred twenty-nine thousandths

161. __________________________  twenty-three million seven hundred forty-six thousand one hundred sixty-six and two hundred sixty-eight thousandths

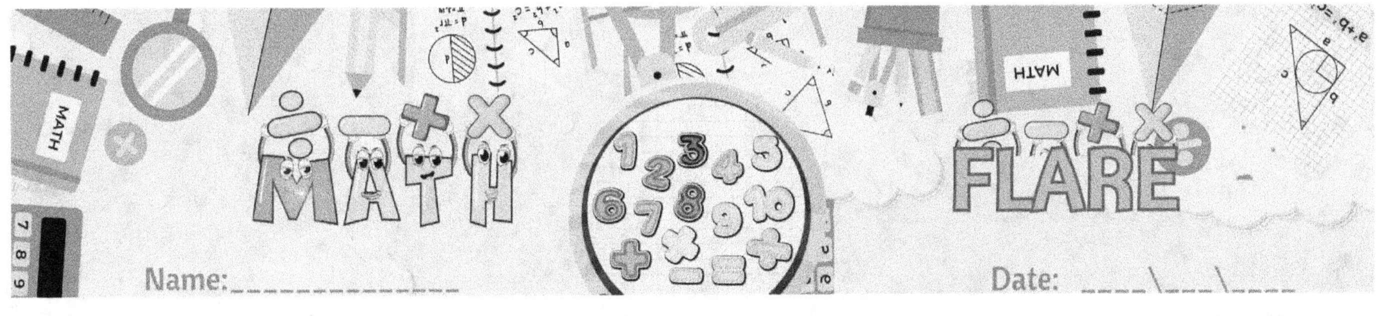


162. _______________________________    twelve million five hundred seven thousand two hundred ninety-nine and twenty-three thousandths

163. _______________________________    thirty-one million nine hundred forty-eight thousand five hundred thirty-two and three hundred eighty-eight thousandths

164. _______________________________    eighty million two hundred twenty-eight thousand five hundred twenty-eight and nine hundred ninety-four thousandths

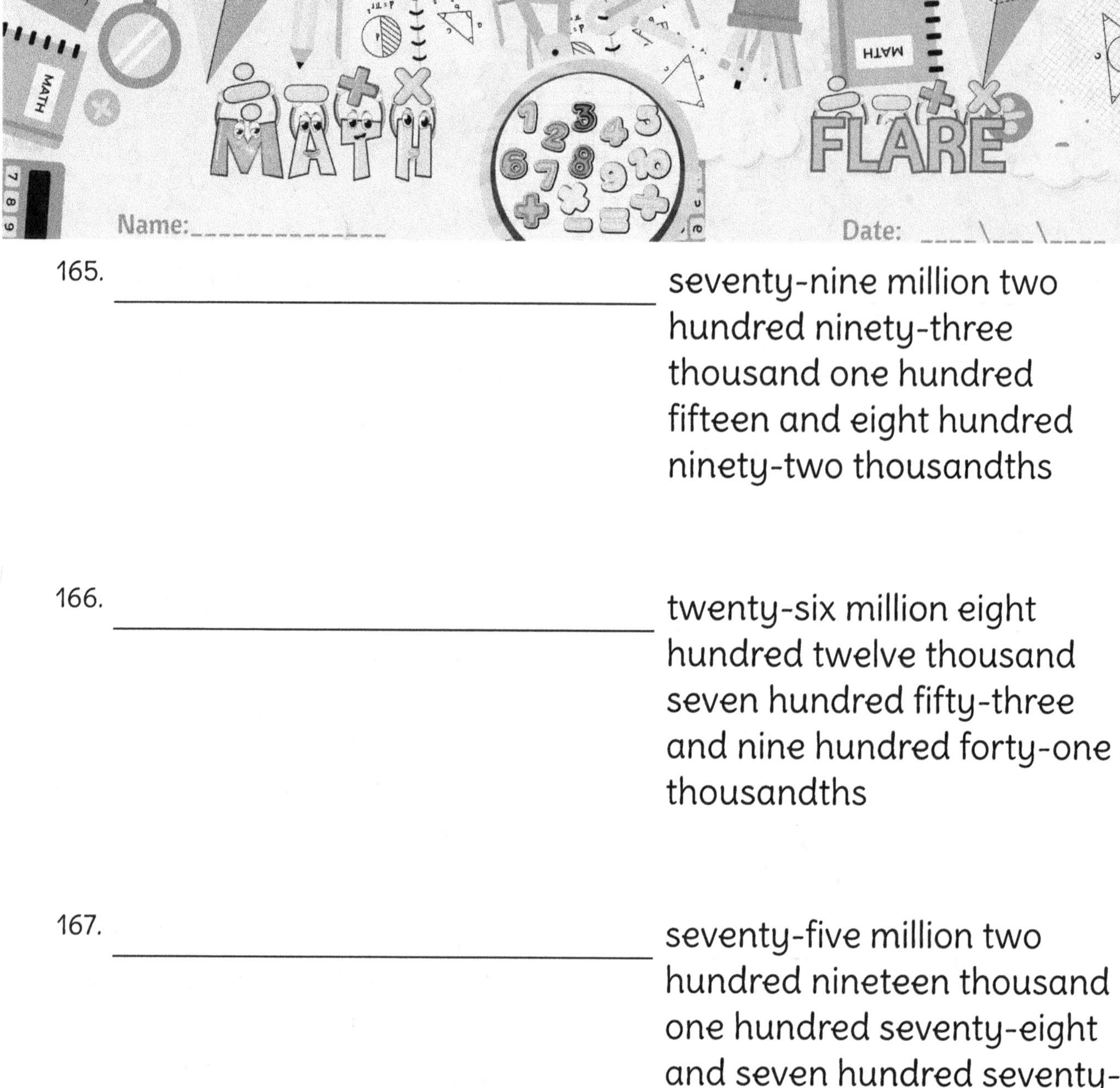


165. _________________________________  seventy-nine million two hundred ninety-three thousand one hundred fifteen and eight hundred ninety-two thousandths

166. _________________________________  twenty-six million eight hundred twelve thousand seven hundred fifty-three and nine hundred forty-one thousandths

167. _________________________________  seventy-five million two hundred nineteen thousand one hundred seventy-eight and seven hundred seventy-four thousandths

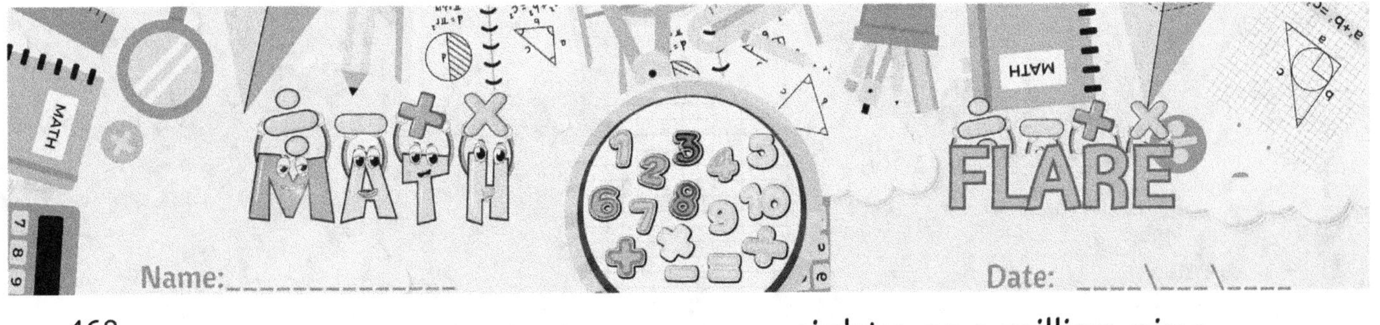


168. _______________________  eighty-one million nine hundred seventy-three thousand nine hundred fifty-six and six hundred eighty-eight thousandths

169. _______________________  fifty-eight million seven hundred forty-nine thousand six hundred twenty-four and two hundred eighty-nine thousandths

170. _______________________  eighty-one million seven hundred ninety thousand four hundred ninety-three and nine hundred twenty-seven thousandths

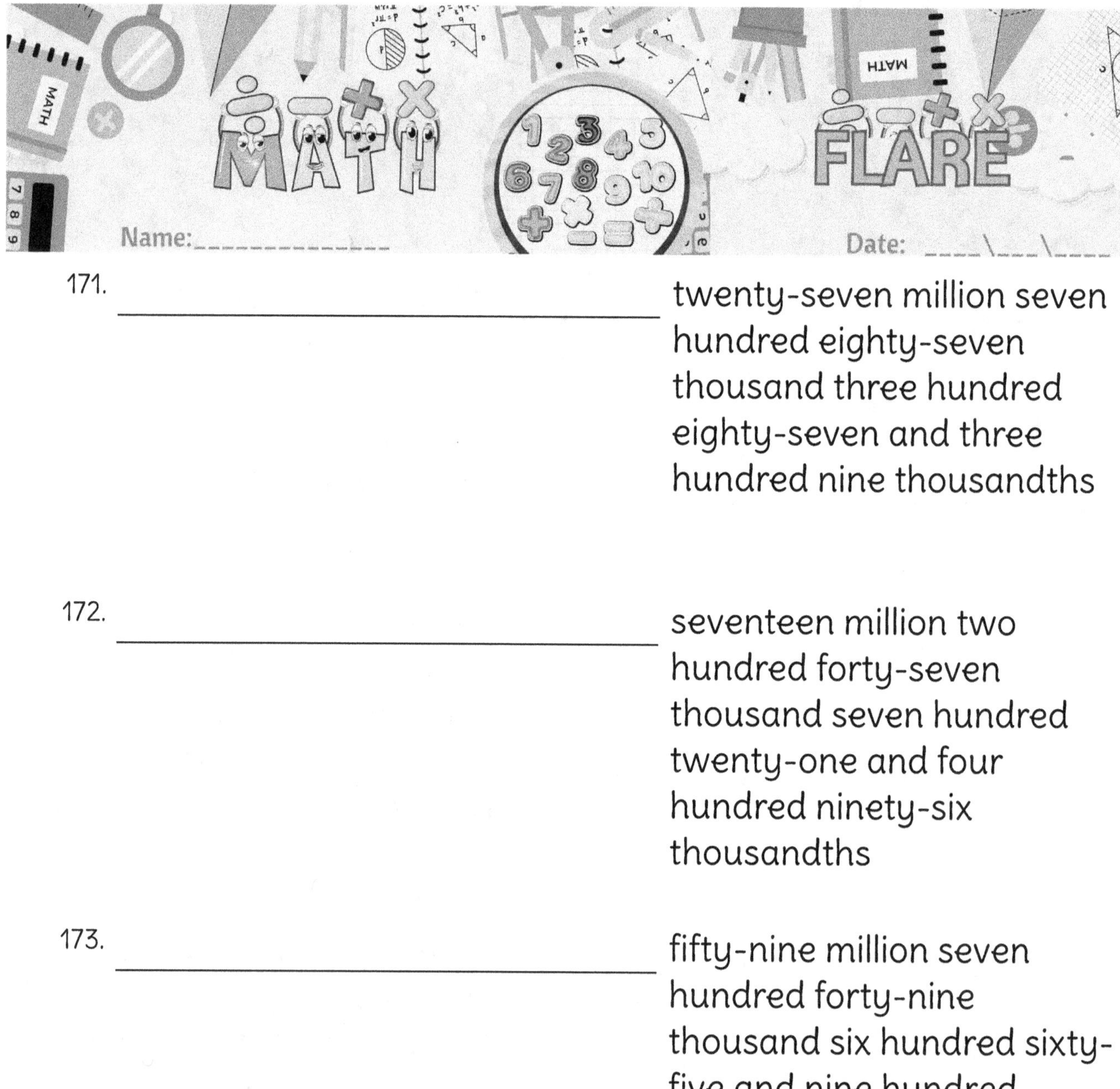


171. _______________________________  twenty-seven million seven hundred eighty-seven thousand three hundred eighty-seven and three hundred nine thousandths

172. _______________________________  seventeen million two hundred forty-seven thousand seven hundred twenty-one and four hundred ninety-six thousandths

173. _______________________________  fifty-nine million seven hundred forty-nine thousand six hundred sixty-five and nine hundred seventy-two thousandths

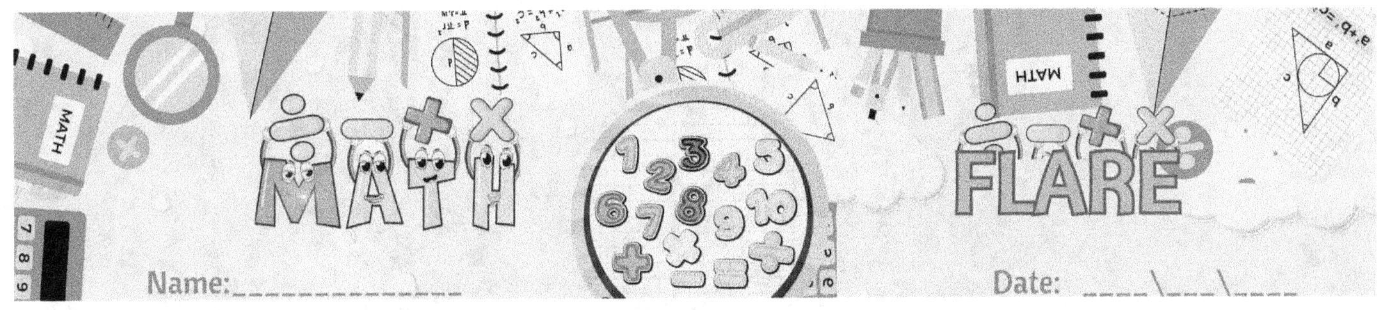


# Place Value: Expanded Notation

Provide the expanded notation for each value.

174. 45,382,999.650

175. 16,935,021.773

176. 43,144,087.155

177. 40,847,311.113

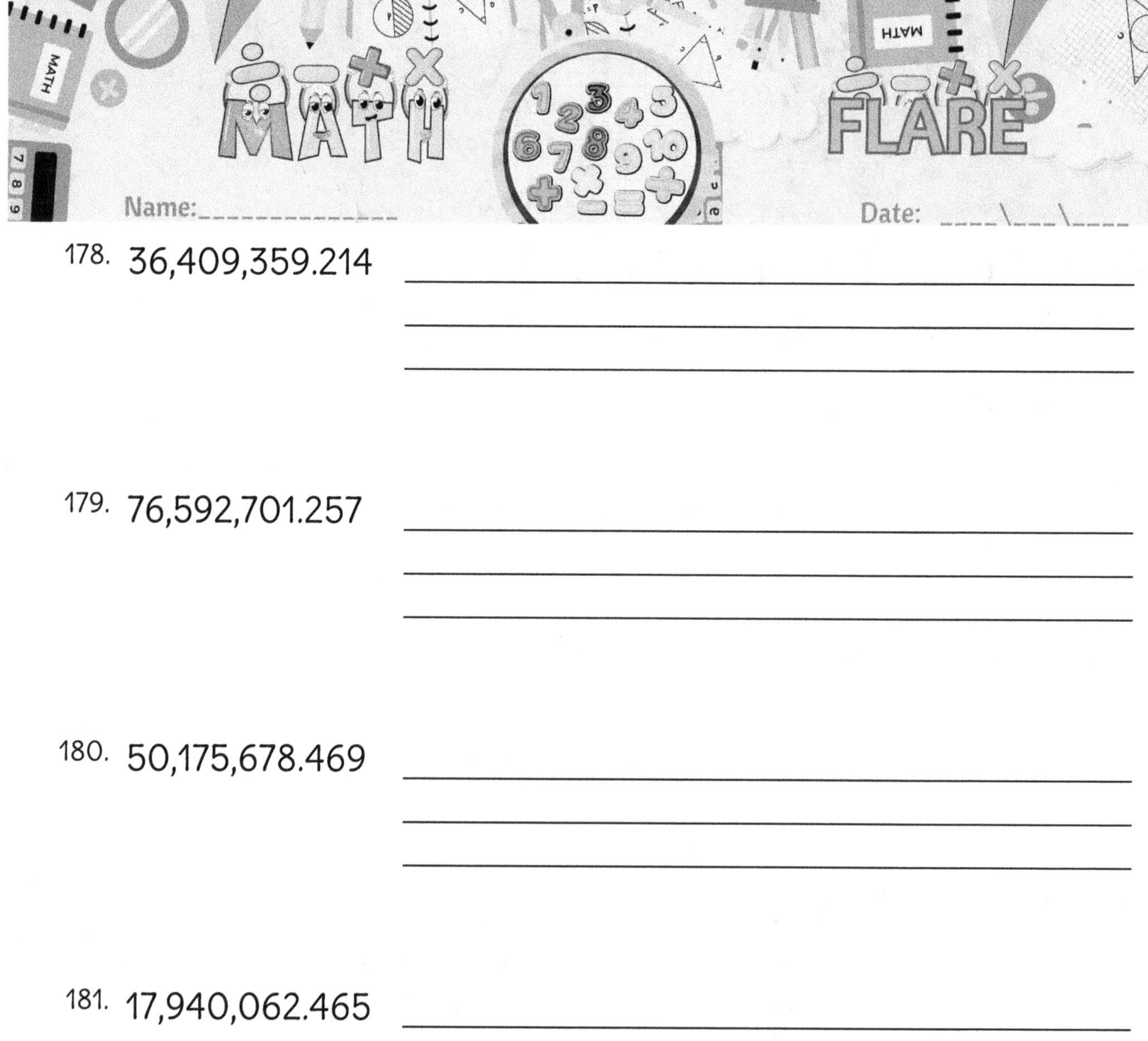



178. 36,409,359.214

179. 76,592,701.257

180. 50,175,678.469

181. 17,940,062.465

182. 34,833,864.967

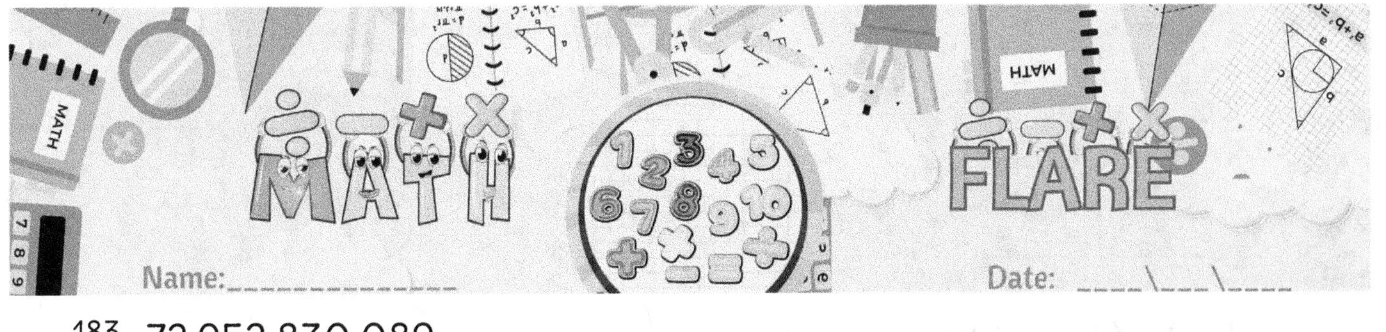



183. 72,952,830.089

184. 82,516,845.893

185. 37,192,353.567

186. 27,710,190.400

187. 71,807,021.788

188.  98,828,987.399  ______________________

189.  52,075,330.122  ______________________

190.  41,206,894.843  ______________________

191.  42,042,450.770  ______________________

192.  49,783,871.266  ______________________

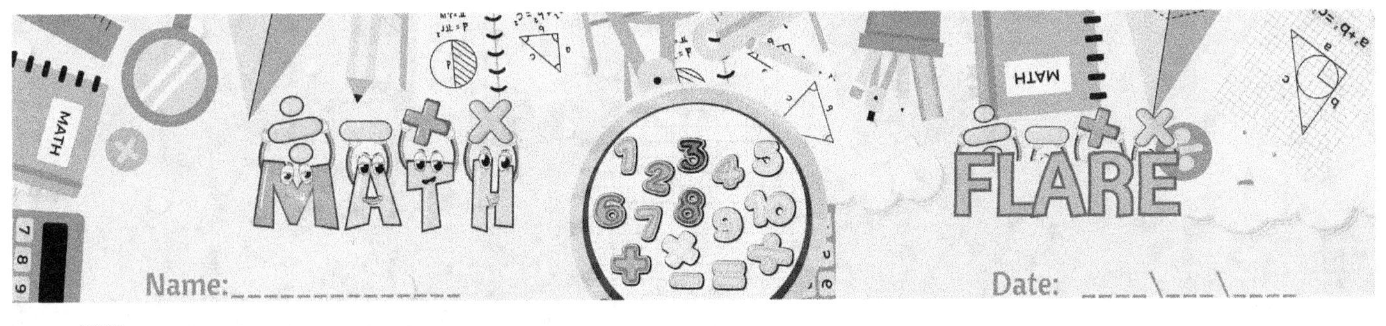


193. 84,626,331.116 _______________________________

194. 51,491,672.346 _______________________________

195. 71,579,980.380 _______________________________

196. 87,400,282.829 _______________________________

197. 97,766,085.298 _______________________________

198. 82,915,868.280 ______________________

199. 89,201,536.890 ______________________

200. 34,146,700.368 ______________________

201. 29,032,671.660 ______________________

202. 89,448,527.814 ______________________

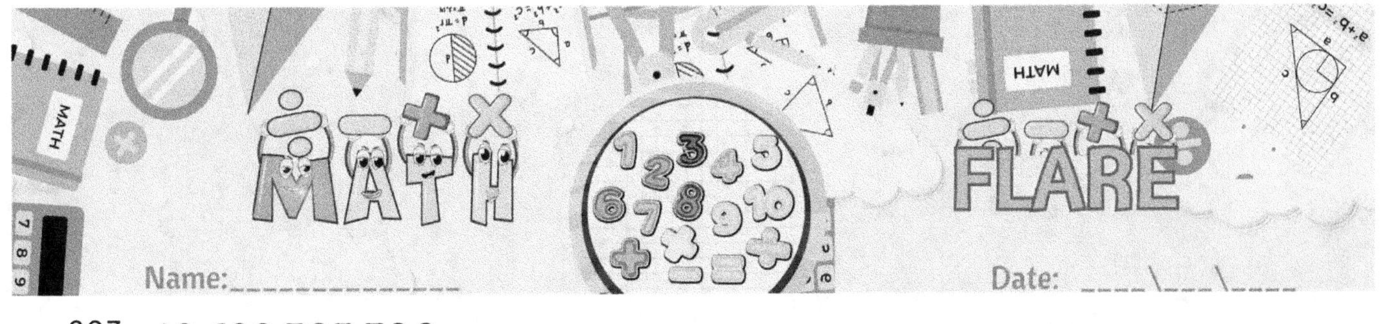


203. 48,629,395.700

204. 87,589,661.412

205. 99,578,721.983

206. 28,038,056.212

207. 16,133,370.351

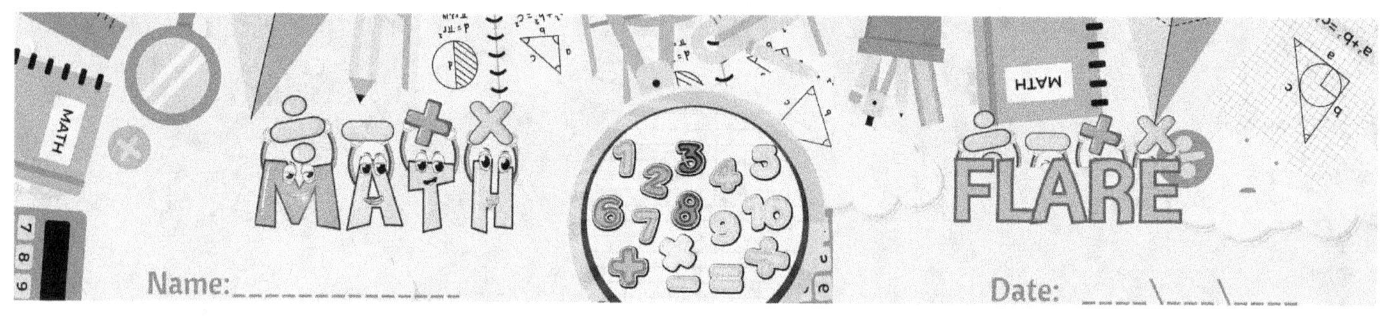


# Rounding Numbers

Round to the underlined digit.

208. 987,112.5451 = _____________

209. 404,313.7362 = _____________

210. 3,335,011.677 = _____________

211. 277,450.8229 = _____________

212. 180,042.0284 = _____________

213. 318,874.0015 = _____________

214. 152,795.2880 = _____________

215. 265,652.1714 = _____________

216. 84,339.50012 = _____________

217. 733,242.6595 = _____________

218. 35,535.86386 = _____________

219. 22,372.90924 = _____________

220. 43,395.17058 = _____________

221. 23,427.96764 = _____________

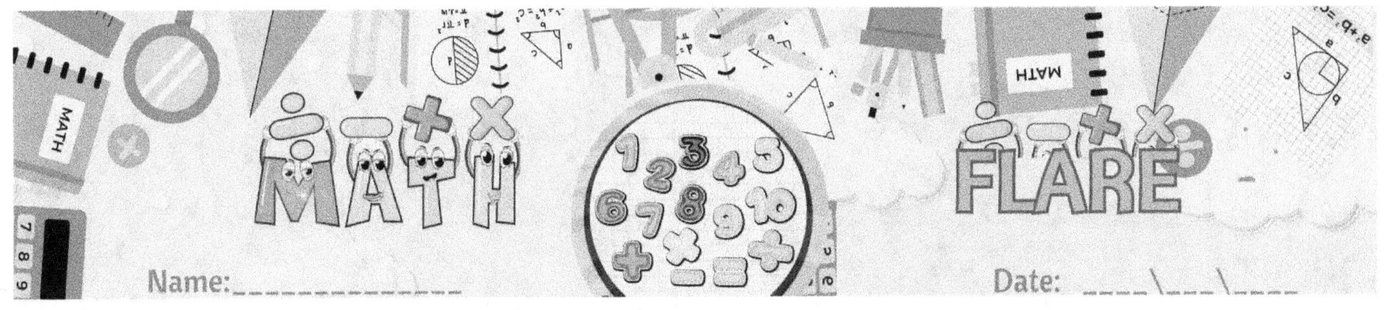


Name:________________    Date: _______________

222. 841,416.7501 = __________

223. 14,653.52561 = __________

224. 8,335,336.292 = __________

225. 1,924,251.437 = __________

226. 661,751.0809 = __________

227. 78,506.95686 = __________

228. 30,476.03300 = __________

229. 6,680,187.777 = __________

230. 32,723.51523 = __________

231. 81,600.35376 = __________

232. 3,072,211.507 = __________

233. 408,492.8928 = __________

234. 777,167.7272 = __________

235. 53,798.26464 = __________

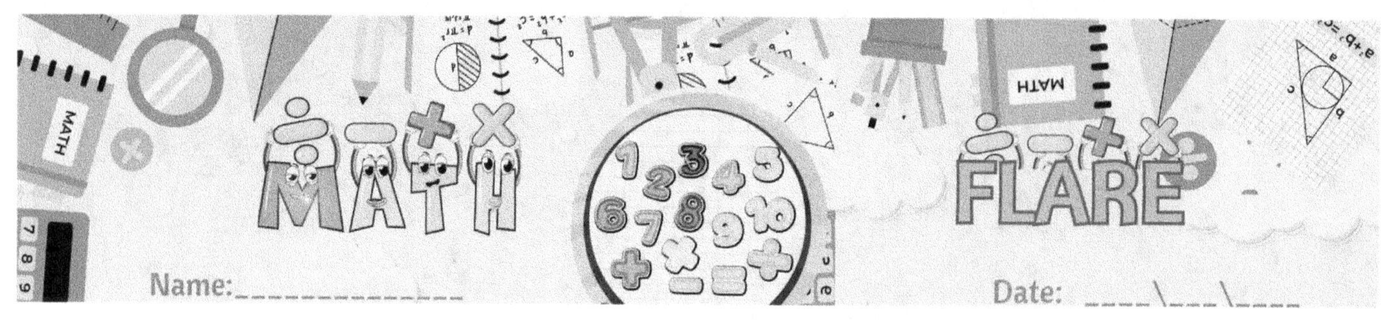


236. 37,16<u>3</u>.21262 = _____________

237. 1,132,2<u>7</u>6.360 = _____________

238. 57,572.9<u>0</u>302 = _____________

239. 16,<u>3</u>49.48683 = _____________

240. 12,84<u>8</u>.79456 = _____________

241. 7<u>8</u>,202.07645 = _____________

242. <u>4</u>,479,068.776 = _____________

243. 172,319.0<u>4</u>13 = _____________

244. 222,663.0<u>1</u>49 = _____________

245. 7,819,89<u>2</u>.380 = _____________

246. 2,9<u>7</u>4,016.422 = _____________

247. 3,468,970.87<u>2</u> = _____________

248. 78<u>4</u>,508.0976 = _____________

249. <u>2</u>,973,569.306 = _____________

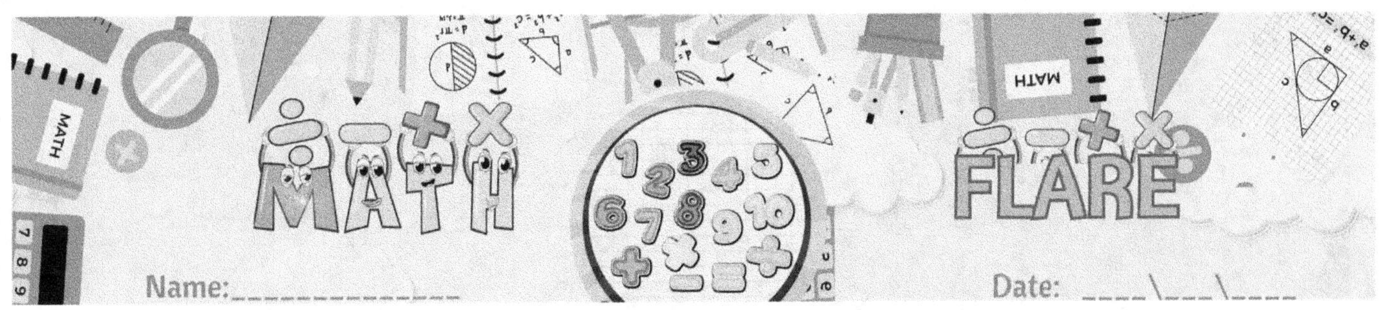



250. 6,720,934.<u>3</u>75 = ______________

251. 14,8<u>6</u>1.48406 = ______________

252. 82,199.10<u>4</u>95 = ______________

253. 185,34<u>3</u>.0164 = ______________

254. 732,038.7<u>2</u>53 = ______________

255. <u>6</u>55,760.6822 = ______________

256. 8,429,0<u>8</u>9.120 = ______________

257. <u>8</u>1,754.54431 = ______________

258. 496,597.<u>6</u>834 = ______________

259. 8,875,750.93<u>3</u> = ______________

260. 3<u>5</u>,769.36138 = ______________

261. 3,275,702.52<u>9</u> = ______________

262. <u>3</u>66,910.1785 = ______________

263. 924,290.4<u>8</u>29 = ______________

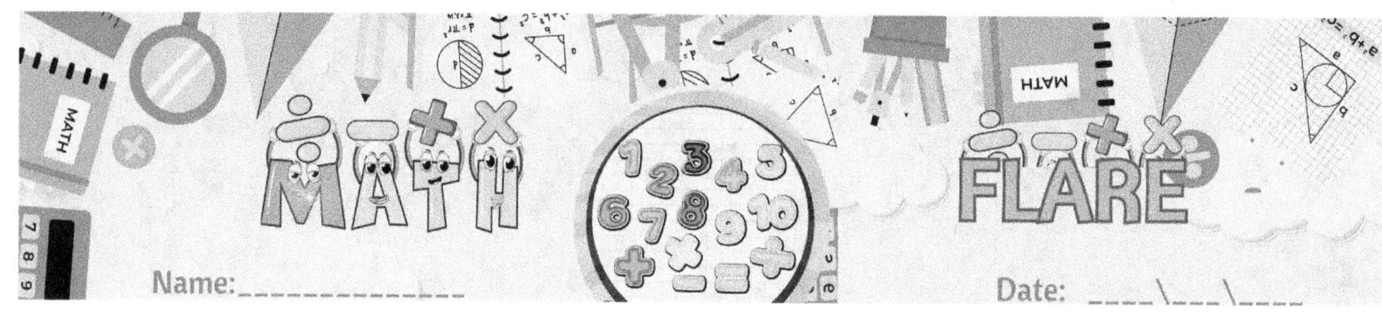


264. 58,328.44094 = _________

265. 948,481.4346 = _________

266. 575,515.8109 = _________

267. 527,362.2604 = _________

268. 44,447.65930 = _________

269. 9,708,305.423 = _________

270. 7,233,340.124 = _________

271. 46,608.99145 = _________

272. 945,992.2646 = _________

273. 606,045.9461 = _________

274. 5,601,502.603 = _________

275. 7,587,355.743 = _________

276. 11,122.26119 = _________

277. 253,710.4811 = _________

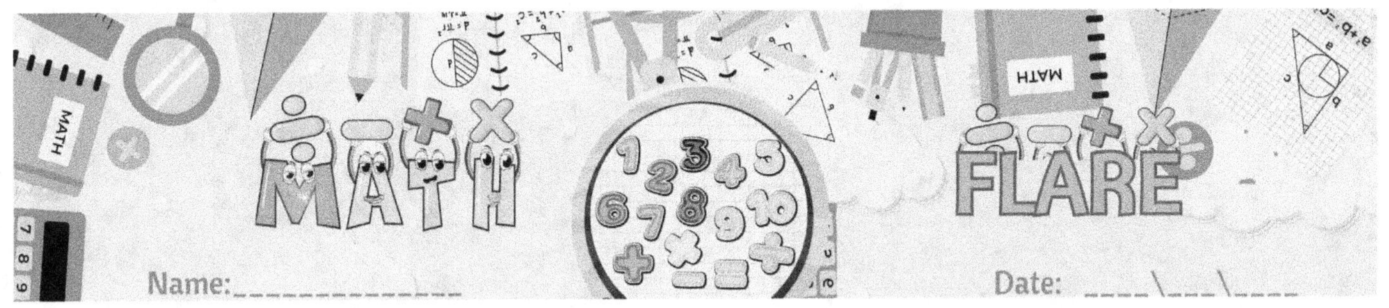



278. 46,8<u>7</u>3.17354 = ___________

279. <u>5</u>1,772.40340 = ___________

280. 146,442.<u>5</u>354 = ___________

281. 348,285.<u>1</u>748 = ___________

282. 2,035,98<u>6</u>.016 = ___________

283. 9,563,7<u>1</u>7.773 = ___________

284. 14,120.0<u>8</u>193 = ___________

285. 4,896,67<u>1</u>.257 = ___________

286. 152,351.40<u>3</u>3 = ___________

287. <u>7</u>,752,101.094 = ___________

288. 8<u>4</u>,427.43383 = ___________

289. 32,9<u>4</u>2.25156 = ___________

290. 58,2<u>9</u>8.18420 = ___________

291. 5<u>3</u>,378.61623 = ___________

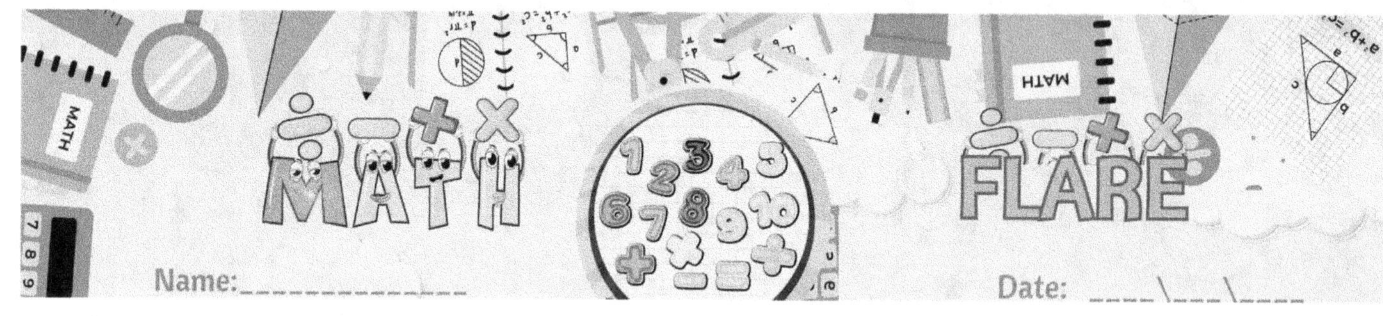


292. 19,915.88039 = __________

293. 665,708.7130 = __________

294. 4,983,802.921 = __________

295. 963,454.2219 = __________

296. 579,662.5178 = __________

297. 430,731.3237 = __________

298. 9,924,642.821 = __________

299. 966,984.3769 = __________

300. 39,372.98723 = __________

301. 68,763.77431 = __________

302. 123,086.2428 = __________

303. 7,089,747.486 = __________

304. 1,236,026.992 = __________

305. 6,174,548.462 = __________

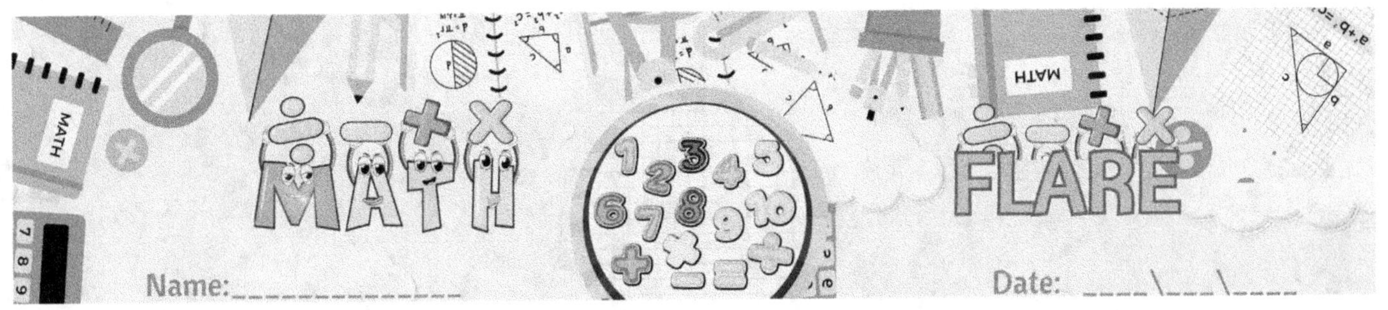


306. 643,777.5<u>4</u>47 = _______________

307. <u>2</u>49,981.4193 = _______________

308. 657,<u>6</u>20.4313 = _______________

309. <u>7</u>,749,855.431 = _______________

310. <u>4</u>13,120.6442 = _______________

311. 792,4<u>3</u>7.8466 = _______________

312. <u>5</u>21,905.2638 = _______________

313. 919,548.6<u>1</u>36 = _______________

314. 1<u>7</u>9,669.9105 = _______________

315. 12,447.98<u>7</u>46 = _______________

316. 290,002.89<u>7</u>3 = _______________

317. <u>7</u>2,307.86564 = _______________

318. 60,<u>7</u>81.41773 = _______________

319. 14,<u>7</u>44.47982 = _______________

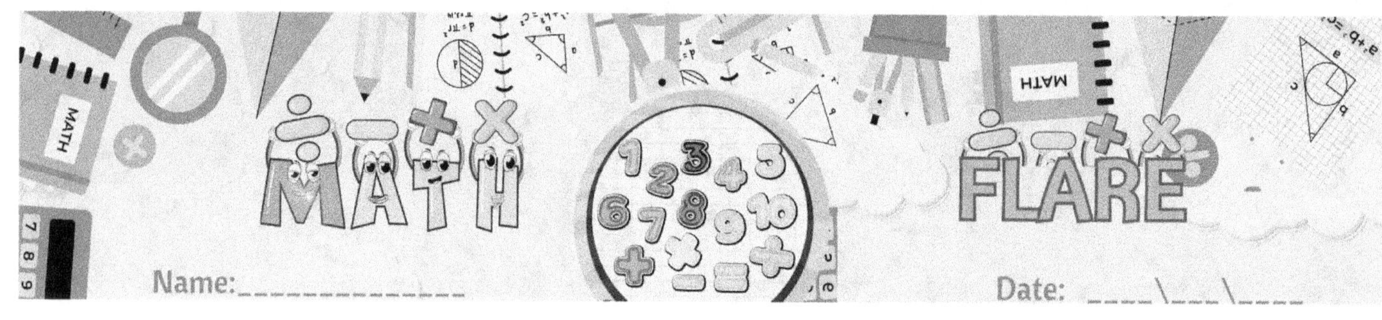


320. 57,818.05_340 = ___________

321. 753,10_0.3030 = ___________

322. _54,817.82295 = ___________

323. _9,274,989.879 = ___________

324. 1,878,858._616 = ___________

325. 974,306.98_73 = ___________

326. _81,696.00242 = ___________

327. 65,404.22_630 = ___________

328. 6,227,_899.607 = ___________

329. _65,288.55105 = ___________

330. 43,997.58_291 = ___________

331. 5,2_11,514.671 = ___________

332. 212,_286.4497 = ___________

333. 12_1,741.5638 = ___________

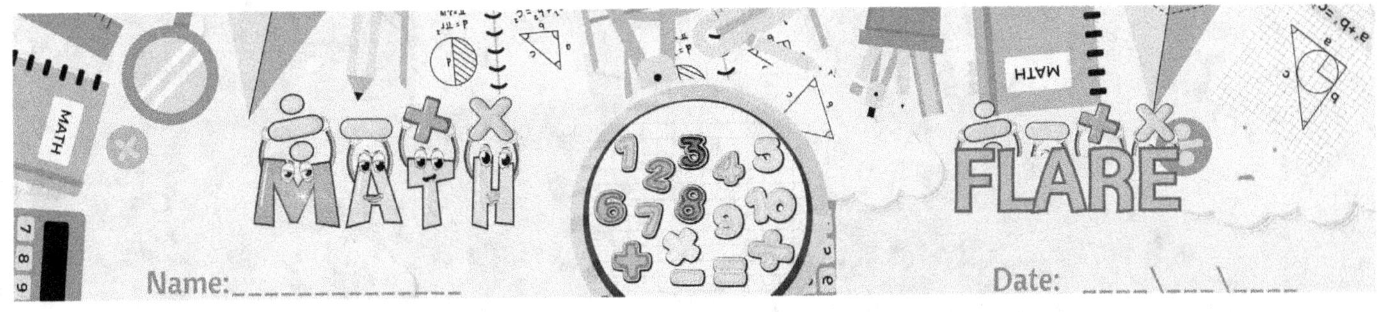


334. 77,783.6<u>8</u>487 = _____________

335. <u>3</u>4,317.64375 = _____________

336. 2,3<u>0</u>3,093.357 = _____________

337. 43,82<u>6</u>.27847 = _____________

338. 52,6<u>5</u>6.84720 = _____________

339. 52,738.951<u>3</u>8 = _____________

340. 99,089.1<u>6</u>049 = _____________

341. 7,265,982.60<u>7</u> = _____________

342. 2<u>6</u>8,975.7033 = _____________

343. 535,36<u>8</u>.7465 = _____________

344. 7,082,173.4<u>5</u>1 = _____________

345. 6,449,64<u>0</u>.739 = _____________

346. 8,061,0<u>9</u>8.773 = _____________

347. 499,658.5<u>3</u>19 = _____________

# ANSWERS

## Page 1:   Place Value

1. 6 ten thousands
2. 9 tens
3. 0 hundred millions
4. 6 thousandths
5. 1 million
6. 6 hundreds
7. 8 ten millions
8. 9 thousands
9. 9 ones
10. 5 tenths
11. 7 tenths
12. 3 tens
13. 0 ten thousands
14. 7 millions
15. 2 tenths
16. 2 hundred millions
17. 0 millions
18. 2 ones
19. 4 tenths
20. 3 hundred thousands
21. 4 millions
22. 6 ten millions
23. 7 tenths
24. 8 tenths
25. 8 ten thousands
26. 3 tenths
27. 5 hundredths
28. 9 tenths
29. 2 ten thousands
30. 4 thousandths

## Page 5:   Place Value: Expanded Notation

31. 99,997,789.314
32. 80,921,073.099
33. 48,870,789.482
34. 98,442,671.013
35. 13,210,386.850
36. 89,412,307.179
37. 62,508,901.493
38. 11,804,622.203
39. 93,446,719.852

40. 20,737,282.089     41. 70,788,183.226     42. 73,050,858.794

43. 48,327,293.721     44. 18,781,206.901     45. 29,276,967.048

46. 16,162,964.504     47. 36,052,572.483     48. 73,030,501.623

49. 68,178,317.829     50. 79,668,048.983     51. 77,835,965.485

52. 75,249,923.008     53. 39,374,967.836     54. 53,019,731.935

55. 77,061,675.613     56. 98,007,353.561     57. 40,764,157.227

58. 15,023,678.078     59. 92,140,592.900     60. 95,370,066.726

61. 13,076,757.017

## Page 13:  Place Value: Expanded Notation

62. 2 ten millions + 2 millions + 9 hundred thousands + 5 ten thousands + 3 thousands + 2 hundreds + 4 tens + 2 ones + 8 tenths + 3 hundredths + 8 thousandths

63. 4 ten millions + 2 millions + 4 hundred thousands + 6 ten thousands + 8 thousands + 7 hundreds + 5 tens + 2 ones + 5 tenths + 2 hundredths + 2 thousandths

64. 5 ten millions + 1 million + 9 hundred thousands + 9 ten thousands + 4 thousands + 3 hundreds + 4 tens + 4 ones + 1 tenth + 7 hundredths + 3 thousandths

65. 3 ten millions + 1 million + 5 hundred thousands + 9 ten thousands + 4 hundreds + 6 tens + 9 ones + 9 tenths + 3 hundredths + 2 thousandths

66. 1 ten million + 4 millions + 4 hundred thousands + 4 thousands + 8 hundreds + 1 ten + 1 tenth + 6 thousandths

67. 8 ten millions + 9 millions + 8 hundred thousands + 4 ten thousands + 2 thousands + 7 hundreds + 6 tens + 5 ones + 9 tenths + 3 hundredths + 6 thousandths

68. 2 ten millions + 6 millions + 2 hundred thousands + 8 ten thousands + 5 thousands + 7 ones + 3 tenths + 9 hundredths + 9 thousandths

69. 3 ten millions + 2 millions + 7 hundred thousands + 5 ten thousands + 5 thousands + 1 hundred + 8 tens + 8 ones + 8 tenths + 5 hundredths + 5 thousandths

70. 9 ten millions + 3 millions + 7 ten thousands + 5 thousands + 6 hundreds + 7 tens + 8 ones + 8 tenths + 5 hundredths + 7 thousandths

71. 3 ten millions + 6 millions + 8 hundred thousands + 4 ten thousands + 7 thousands + 7 hundreds + 7 tens + 3 tenths + 8 hundredths + 5 thousandths

72. 4 ten millions + 1 million + 8 hundred thousands + 7 ten thousands + 6 thousands + 9 hundreds + 1 ten + 4 ones + 2 tenths + 6 hundredths

73. 4 ten millions + 4 hundred thousands + 9 thousands + 6 hundreds + 3 tens + 8 ones + 5 tenths + 5 hundredths + 6 thousandths

74. 1 ten million + 7 millions + 5 hundred thousands + 4 ten thousands + 3 thousands + 4 hundreds + 8 tens + 2 tenths + 6 hundredths

75. 2 ten millions + 3 hundred thousands + 1 ten thousand + 3 thousands + 7 tens + 1 one + 6 tenths + 6 hundredths + 4 thousandths

76. 2 ten millions + 4 millions + 1 hundred thousand + 7 ten thousands + 5 thousands + 3 hundreds + 3 tens + 2 ones + 9 tenths + 9 hundredths + 6 thousandths

77. 4 ten millions + 3 millions + 7 hundred thousands + 6 ten thousands + 3 thousands + 7 hundreds + 7 tens + 4 ones + 5 tenths + 8 hundredths + 4 thousandths

78. 7 ten millions + 6 millions + 3 hundred thousands + 6 ten thousands + 7 thousands + 8 hundreds + 5 tens + 7 ones + 7 tenths + 1 hundredth

79. 2 ten millions + 8 millions + 9 hundred thousands + 6 ten thousands + 9 hundreds + 3 tens + 9 ones + 1 tenth + 6 hundredths + 5 thousandths

80. 7 ten millions + 9 millions + 8 hundred thousands + 5 ten thousands + 5 thousands + 5 hundreds + 8 tens + 3 ones + 5 tenths + 8 hundredths + 9 thousandths

81. 6 ten millions + 6 millions + 6 hundred thousands + 7 ten thousands + 3 thousands + 5 hundreds + 6 tens + 8 ones + 9 tenths + 4 hundredths + 1 thousandth

82. 2 ten millions + 2 millions + 7 hundred thousands + 8 ten thousands + 2 thousands + 3 hundreds + 4 tens + 1 one + 2 tenths + 3 hundredths + 8 thousandths

83. 9 ten millions + 4 hundred thousands + 4 thousands + 8 tens + 1 tenth + 5 hundredths + 6 thousandths

84. 6 ten millions + 7 millions + 7 hundred thousands + 6 ten thousands + 9 thousands + 6 hundreds + 8 tens + 2 ones + 5 tenths + 7 hundredths + 3 thousandths

85. 3 ten millions + 1 million + 2 hundred thousands + 8 ten thousands + 5 thousands + 1 hundred + 9 tens + 7 ones + 8 tenths + 7 hundredths + 5 thousandths

86. 3 ten millions + 4 millions + 7 hundred thousands + 4 ten thousands + 7 thousands + 8 hundreds + 6 tens + 6 ones + 3 tenths + 6 thousandths

87. 5 ten millions + 1 million + 5 hundred thousands + 4 ten thousands + 6 thousands + 1 hundred + 5 ones + 2 tenths + 6 hundredths + 3 thousandths

88. 9 ten millions + 5 millions + 8 hundred thousands + 5 ten thousands + 1 thousand + 5 tens + 7 ones + 5 tenths + 4 hundredths + 6 thousandths

89. 3 ten millions + 1 million + 3 hundred thousands + 8 ten thousands + 9 hundreds + 9 tens + 5 ones + 4 tenths + 1 thousandth

## Page 20:   Place Value: Expanded Notation

90. 15,203,033.288     91. 58,648,149.952     92. 57,485,223.415

93. 19,664,029.302     94. 98,076,653.125     95. 17,660,525.072

96. 57,834,940.388     97. 40,582,106.272     98. 96,332,949.546

99. 87,190,736.968     100. 24,872,156.943     101. 26,320,198.568

102. 19,767,565.084     103. 50,275,312.769     104. 75,102,638.972

105. 52,820,278.598     106. 45,959,051.226     107. 44,840,284.453

108. 31,831,487.576     109. 42,706,660.271     110. 62,886,342.617

111. 64,243,578.977     112. 64,396,299.516     113. 86,062,738.911

114. 22,285,009.312     115. 38,696,497.785     116. 90,294,415.778

117. 32,549,162.680

## Page 27:   Place Value: Expanded Notation

118. 7,000,000 + 400,000 + 60,000 + 9,000 + 900 + 6 + 0.9 + 0.09 + 0.004

119. 3,000,000 + 70,000 + 900 + 10 + 4 + 0.6 + 0.03

120. 9,000,000 + 600,000 + 80,000 + 4,000 + 200 + 60 + 0.3 + 0.06 + 0.002

121. 6,000,000 + 200,000 + 80,000 + 5,000 + 800 + 70 + 0.4 + 0.08 + 0.004

122. 9,000,000 + 300,000 + 90,000 + 9,000 + 100 + 70 + 0.8 + 0.03 + 0.008

123. 9,000,000 + 400,000 + 90,000 + 400 + 1 + 0.1 + 0.09 + 0.009

124. 2,000,000 + 700,000 + 50,000 + 5,000 + 200 + 10 + 5 + 0.5 + 0.05 + 0.007

125. 4,000,000 + 400,000 + 40,000 + 2,000 + 700 + 50 + 2 + 0.8 + 0.09

126. 7,000,000 + 900,000 + 30,000 + 6,000 + 200 + 50 + 4 + 0.6 + 0.09 + 0.006

127. 3,000,000 + 200,000 + 20,000 + 1,000 + 200 + 80 + 8 + 0.4 + 0.09 + 0.006

128. 4,000,000 + 200,000 + 30,000 + 3,000 + 200 + 90 + 8 + 0.5 + 0.04 + 0.003

129. 9,000,000 + 900,000 + 80,000 + 8,000 + 200 + 90 + 5 + 0.5 + 0.01 + 0.008

130. 6,000,000 + 200,000 + 40,000 + 7,000 + 800 + 10 + 3 + 0.1 + 0.02 + 0.007

131. 8,000,000 + 300,000 + 50,000 + 9,000 + 300 + 20 + 2 + 0.6 + 0.07 + 0.002

132. 4,000,000 + 700,000 + 40,000 + 3,000 + 80 + 2 + 0.5 + 0.003

133. 8,000,000 + 900,000 + 10,000 + 7,000 + 700 + 10 + 2 + 0.07 + 0.003

134. 1,000,000 + 400,000 + 8,000 + 800 + 70 + 8 + 0.2 + 0.02 + 0.002

135. 6,000,000 + 300,000 + 50,000 + 3,000 + 500 + 30 + 8 + 0.5 + 0.002

136. 5,000,000 + 600,000 + 90,000 + 600 + 0.3 + 0.08 + 0.005

137. 7,000,000 + 200,000 + 50,000 + 700 + 2 + 0.8 + 0.04 + 0.006

138. 2,000,000 + 500,000 + 30,000 + 100 + 40 + 4 + 0.1 + 0.01 + 0.008

139. 2,000,000 + 400,000 + 90,000 + 4,000 + 900 + 40 + 0.3 + 0.09 + 0.007

140. 8,000,000 + 500,000 + 30,000 + 2,000 + 600 + 10 + 4 + 0.6 + 0.06 + 0.004

141. 8,000,000 + 900,000 + 90,000 + 700 + 50 + 8 + 0.1 + 0.08 + 0.004

142. 2,000,000 + 900,000 + 70,000 + 1,000 + 400 + 60 + 1 + 0.7 + 0.06 + 0.008

143. 6,000,000 + 300,000 + 10,000 + 4,000 + 400 + 30 + 9 + 0.7 + 0.02 + 0.007

144. 6,000,000 + 800,000 + 40,000 + 9,000 + 400 + 60 + 5 + 0.2 + 0.07 + 0.008

145. 5,000,000 + 90,000 + 5,000 + 900 + 40 + 5 + 0.4 + 0.03 + 0.001

146. 9,000,000 + 400,000 + 20,000 + 5,000 + 100 + 80 + 5 + 0.04 + 0.003

## Page 32:  Place Value: Expanded Notation

147. 71,422,484.503

148. 97,379,019.989

149. 69,380,155.340

150. 27,366,109.293

151. 35,285,777.708

152. 65,883,036.323

153. 75,623,803.248

154. 90,348,133.342

155. 62,013,452.100

156. 32,328,490.178

157. 24,863,553.087

158. 32,723,157.202

159. 40,675,110.067

160. 73,457,731.629

161. 23,746,166.268

162. 12,507,299.023

163. 31,948,532.388

164. 80,228,528.994

165. 79,293,115.892     166. 26,812,753.941     167. 75,219,178.774

168. 81,973,956.688     169. 58,749,624.289     170. 81,790,493.927

171. 27,787,387.309     172. 17,247,721.496     173. 59,749,665.972

## Page 41:  Place Value: Expanded Notation

174. forty-five million three hundred eighty-two thousand nine hundred ninety-nine and six hundred fifty thousandths

175. sixteen million nine hundred thirty-five thousand twenty-one and seven hundred seventy-three thousandths

176. forty-three million one hundred forty-four thousand eighty-seven and one hundred fifty-five thousandth

177. forty million eight hundred forty-seven thousand three hundred eleven and one hundred thirteen thousandth

178. thirty-six million four hundred nine thousand three hundred fifty-nine and two hundred fourteen thousandths

179. seventy-six million five hundred ninety-two thousand seven hundred one and two hundred fifty-seven thousandths

180. fifty million one hundred seventy-five thousand six hundred seventy-eight and four hundred sixty-nine thousandths

181. seventeen million nine hundred forty thousand sixty-two and four hundred sixty-five thousandths

182. thirty-four million eight hundred thirty-three thousand eight hundred sixty-four and nine hundred sixty-seven thousandths

183. seventy-two million nine hundred fifty-two thousand eight hundred thirty and eighty-nine thousandths

184. eighty-two million five hundred sixteen thousand eight hundred forty-five and eight hundred ninety-three thousandths

185. thirty-seven million one hundred ninety-two thousand three hundred fifty-three and five hundred sixty-seven thousandths

186. twenty-seven million seven hundred ten thousand one hundred ninety and four hundred thousandths

187. seventy-one million eight hundred seven thousand twenty-one and seven hundred eighty-eight thousandths

188. ninety-eight million eight hundred twenty-eight thousand nine hundred eighty-seven and three hundred ninety-nine thousandths

189. fifty-two million seventy-five thousand three hundred thirty and one hundred twenty-two thousandth

190. forty-one million two hundred six thousand eight hundred ninety-four and eight hundred forty-three thousandths

191. forty-two million forty-two thousand four hundred fifty and seven hundred seventy thousandths

192. forty-nine million seven hundred eighty-three thousand eight hundred seventy-one and two hundred sixty-six thousandths

193. eighty-four million six hundred twenty-six thousand three hundred thirty-one and one hundred sixteen thousandth

194. fifty-one million four hundred ninety-one thousand six hundred seventy-two and three hundred forty-six thousandths

195. seventy-one million five hundred seventy-nine thousand nine hundred eighty and three hundred eighty thousandths

196. eighty-seven million four hundred thousand two hundred eighty-two and eight hundred twenty-nine thousandths

197. ninety-seven million seven hundred sixty-six thousand eighty-five and two hundred ninety-eight thousandths

198. eighty-two million nine hundred fifteen thousand eight hundred sixty-eight and two hundred eighty thousandths

199. eighty-nine million two hundred one thousand five hundred thirty-six and eight hundred ninety thousandths

200. thirty-four million one hundred forty-six thousand seven hundred and three hundred sixty-eight thousandths

201. twenty-nine million thirty-two thousand six hundred seventy-one and six hundred sixty thousandths

202. eighty-nine million four hundred forty-eight thousand five hundred twenty-seven and eight hundred fourteen thousandths

203. forty-eight million six hundred twenty-nine thousand three hundred ninety-five and seven hundred thousandths

204. eighty-seven million five hundred eighty-nine thousand six hundred sixty-one and four hundred twelve thousandths

205. ninety-nine million five hundred seventy-eight thousand seven hundred twenty-one and nine hundred eighty-three thousandths

206. twenty-eight million thirty-eight thousand fifty-six and two hundred twelve thousandths

207. sixteen million one hundred thirty-three thousand three hundred seventy and three hundred fifty-one thousandths

## Page 48:   Rounding Numbers

| | | |
|---|---|---|
| 208. 987,112.55 | 209. 404,314 | 210. 3,335,000 |
| 211. 300,000 | 212. 180,042.03 | 213. 318,874.002 |
| 214. 152,795.288 | 215. 265,652.2 | 216. 84,300 |
| 217. 700,000 | 218. 35,535.9 | 219. 22,372.909 |
| 220. 40,000 | 221. 23,427.968 | 222. 840,000 |
| 223. 14,650 | 224. 8,000,000 | 225. 1,924,251.4 |
| 226. 661,751.08 | 227. 78,507 | 228. 30,500 |
| 229. 6,680,187.8 | 230. 32,700 | 231. 81,600 |
| 232. 3,072,200 | 233. 408,000 | 234. 777,167.727 |
| 235. 54,000 | 236. 37,163 | 237. 1,132,280 |
| 238. 57,572.9 | 239. 16,300 | 240. 12,849 |
| 241. 78,000 | 242. 4,000,000 | 243. 172,319.04 |
| 244. 222,663.01 | 245. 7,819,892 | 246. 2,970,000 |
| 247. 3,468,970.872 | 248. 785,000 | 249. 3,000,000 |
| 250. 6,720,934.4 | 251. 14,860 | 252. 82,199.105 |
| 253. 185,343 | 254. 732,038.73 | 255. 700,000 |
| 256. 8,429,090 | 257. 80,000 | 258. 496,598 |
| 259. 8,875,750.933 | 260. 36,000 | 261. 3,275,702.529 |
| 262. 400,000 | 263. 924,290.48 | 264. 58,328.4 |
| 265. 948,481 | 266. 580,000 | 267. 500,000 |

268. 44,450

269. 9,708,305.423

270. 7,200,000

271. 46,609

272. 946,000

273. 606,045.9

274. 6,000,000

275. 7,587,356

276. 11,122.261

277. 253,700

278. 46,900

279. 50,000

280. 146,442.5

281. 348,285.2

282. 2,035,986

283. 9,563,720

284. 14,120.08

285. 4,896,671

286. 152,351.403

287. 8,000,000

288. 84,000

289. 32,940

290. 58,300

291. 53,000

292. 19,900

293. 665,708.71

294. 4,983,800

295. 963,500

296. 579,700

297. 400,000

298. 9,924,643

299. 970,000

300. 39,372.99

301. 69,000

302. 123,100

303. 7,089,747

304. 1,236,000

305. 6,174,548.462

306. 643,777.54

307. 200,000

308. 658,000

309. 8,000,000

310. 400,000

311. 792,440

312. 500,000

313. 919,548.61

314. 180,000

315. 12,448

316. 290,002.897

317. 70,000

318. 60,800

319. 14,700

320. 57,818.053

321. 753,100

322. 50,000

323. 9,000,000

324. 1,878,858.6

325. 974,306.987

326. 80,000

327. 65,404.226

328. 6,227,900

329. 70,000

330. 43,997.58

331. 5,200,000

332. 212,000

333. 120,000

334. 77,783.7

335. 30,000

336. 2,300,000

337. 43,826

338. 52,700

339. 52,738.951

340. 99,089.2

341. 7,265,982.607

342. 270,000

343. 535,369

344. 7,082,173.5

345. 6,449,641

346. 8,061,100

347. 499,658.53